Whispers of Heaven

A 90-Day Devotional from
A Company of Women International

ROSALIE STORMENT
AND
FAYE HIGBEE

14 13 12 11   10 9 8 7 6 5 4 3 2 1

Whispers of Heaven: A 90-Day Devotional from
A Company of Women International

Copyright © 2011 by Rosalie Storment and Faye Higbee
Rosalie Storment – rosalieacw@gmail.com
Faye Higbee – mdnf.higbee@gmail.com

Published by Word and Spirit Books

Dedication

To those who listen with their hearts for the whispers of Heaven. May the Voice of the Living God draw you into eternal friendships and great joy!

Introduction

The Voice of God is a soft, gentle whisper that carries the sound of a rushing brook. The Bible describes it as the "voice of many waters." It blends in with the background of our daily lives, and unless we seek His Face, we pass by Him unaware that His desire is to tell us the secrets of His Kingdom. Like sitting on a rock beside a rushing stream, listening for God's direction and moving in cooperation with Him takes a quieting of the mind. Knowing God intimately is a process of hearing His Voice amidst our daily routines and experiences, so that no matter what happens to us at any given moment, we are available to hear Him.

We have collected these daily devotionals from PraiseNet (praisenet@acompanyofwomen.org), the prayer family of A Company of Women International. We pray that they will minister to your heart, encourage your faith, stretch your "tent pegs," and enable you to move forward into the purpose and plan of God for your life!

Day One

"Thou art my hiding place; thou shalt preserve me from trouble;
thou shalt compass me about with songs of deliverance. *Selah.*"

PSALM 32:7 KJV

EXCERPT FROM *WHEN GOD SPEAKS TO MY HEART:*

"My Child,

> *My heart croons over you like a song of love, the melody sweet, with the fragrance of Heaven. Can you not hear it within, eliminating all stress and fear? Listen with your spirit. Open your heart to rejoice in the love I have for you. My heart yearns after you, that you would know Me more intimately. Bask in the warmth of my love, positioned in the assurance of my promises. My love is a shield to you. My hand is upon you to bless you. The beauty of my love is real, and in Me there is a place of quiet, safe rest."*

SONGS IN THE NIGHT

All of us have been in the midst of some very hot fires. At one point I had a hard time sleeping (which makes for a cranky lady) from a difficult trial my family was going through. The temptation for any of us is to wallow—to cry and whine and complain. Personally, I had been trying very hard not to gripe at the Lord about the situation. Worry is another temptation; let's just say that none of us are as good at dumping that one into Jesus' arms as we should be.

One evening, I was awakened in the middle of the night by the sound of singing. What were the voices singing? *Songs of deliverance.* I could hear the Voice of the Holy Spirit whispering those words—*songs of deliverance.* I had never heard the songs before, they were totally new and totally soothing. I was literally surrounded by Heaven singing to me about God's love and protection. For the first time in weeks, I was able to sleep through to the time when I had to get up. Normally, I cat-napped all night and couldn't get back to sleep. But now, I actually awoke refreshed the next day!

In today's excerpt, the Lord reminds us to quiet ourselves and listen to His songs. They are sung over us, infused into us, and meant to give us His comfort. There are even fragrances of Heaven that can waft through the room as we quietly absorb His love into our hearts. God's manifest Presence is available to all, if we dump those complaints and worries into His arms and let Him surround us—He is our "hiding place" and sings to us of His deliverance.

May all of us dwell there today!

Love, Faye

Day Two

"So don't be afraid, little flock. For it gives your Father
great happiness to give you the Kingdom."

LUKE 12:32 NLT

EXCERPT FROM *WHEN GOD SPEAKS TO MY HEART*:

"Eye hath not seen nor ear heard the wondrous works I bring to pass for those who love Me. Don't restrain your thinking as to what you can see. Let your thinking scan the far vistas of my creative power. Handle each situation as it arises with confidence and assurance. Trust Me to make a way for each task that I lay before you. Through trust and perseverance, each task shall be completed well and in my time. Move forward with a renewed and refreshed spirit, and be alive to my ways and leadings. Respond with alertness, trust, peace, and joy. Your days will build beautifully one upon the other, as a patch-work quilt is sewn together to become perfect and whole. Just as each square of the quilt is different, so will each day be different but complete in every way. Rest and be confident in my love and protection for you. Rejoice as each day unfolds to make your life whole and complete."

ANGELS

We mostly have no idea what God has in store for each of us. Angelic encounters, miracles, healings—we simply are "scratching the surface" of the wonders He has promised. As heart friends, we not only pray that you experience the voice of God and His Presence, but that all of His Kingdom will be yours!

As believers in Christ, we have access to the heavenly realms. We must have eyes to see. We can be closed off, afraid, or our minds refuse to believe. But God is able to get past the "educated idiot boxes" of our brains. HE LOVES TO GIVE US HIS KINGDOM! He gets great joy from it!

At one point in my life, I was severely depressed in spite of my love for the Lord. It had become necessary to move home with my mother, who was slowly dying. I was single, very lonely, had no social life, and was in a constant state of working—from 5:30 a.m. to whenever I'd get to bed. One afternoon, I went out jogging on my lunch hour. As I passed a nearby Catholic church, I jogged past a sad-looking elderly man. He was dressed all in black, in the specific uniform of a Catholic priest. But he was dragging his rosary on the sidewalk behind him in a dejected manner.

As I passed him and smiled, the Lord immediately told me to go back and give the man a hug and tell him Jesus loved him. I made a U-turn and obeyed. As I hugged the man and chit-chatted for a moment, tears welled up in his eyes. Then I started to leave and the man vanished! He did not go into the church, he was not walking along the street, he was simply gone. I was left with an odd combination of fear and awe, excitement and joy.

I called my pastor, who started laughing. "What's the matter, can't Catholics have angels?" he remarked. And then it hit me. An ANGEL. The minute he said it, I literally began to tremble from my head to my toes—and cried with overwhelming joy. God was still with me. In the midst of my struggle, the Lord gave me an encounter that lifted my heart and my eyes to His Kingdom and got me out of my self-pity.

GOD WANTS TO GIVE YOU THE KINGDOM. He is Emmanuel, God with us. He lives IN us. His Heavenly Host are the messengers that lift our heads when we are struggling. They are sent to minister to the saints. And they don't always look like the scary ones in Ezekiel or Isaiah. Sometimes they look like a guy in a knit cap who miraculously opens doors, a priest who disappears, or a homeless person with a grocery cart.

God's Kingdom is as close as you desire it to be. In Luke 1:38, Mary says, "I am the Lord's servant. May everything you have said about me come true."

May everything God says about you come true! May every portion of His Kingdom be revealed in your life, including those wonderful encounters with His angelic host.

Love, Faye

Day Three

"Arise, shine; for your light has come!
And the Glory of the LORD is risen upon you.
For behold the darkness shall cover the earth,
and deep darkness the people; but the LORD will
arise over you, and His glory will be seen upon you."

ISAIAH 60:1-2 NKJV

EXCERPT FROM ROSALIE'S JOURNAL:

11/8/09

> *"Seasons of change have rearranged all you have seen and known. Blessings galore have come through your door, causing your heart to soar.*
>
> *Now, my child, you will see and know My Presence wherever you go, in a brand new way, starting today!* **(Wow! That's exciting, Father! What does that mean, Father?)** *Wait and see and you will know that it is Me!*
>
> *Seasons have come and gone but this season calls forth the "New Dawn" bringing forth promises fulfilled.*
>
> *Sing and shout and laugh, my child! The dawn of the new day has arrived to the Glory of God your Father! Seek Me every day as you walk this brand new way!*

11/10/09

> *"Strike out along the trail ahead unencumbered by doubt, unbelief, or weariness.* **(Father, how do I get rid of the weariness?)** *By coming to Me every day and resting in My Presence. My Presence brings peace, joy, hope, and a release from weariness. Seek Me every day in such a way that brings life and energy to all that you do, knowing that I will always bring you through, because I love you!*

11/11/09

> *"Patience and perseverance wins out as one walks step by step in My Presence, knowing that I will make a way into each new day.*
>
> *The tide has turned, my child. Strength of character and resolution has made it so.*

Soooo—here we go!!! Here we go into the wild blue yonder—heading out into the sun (Son), as through open doors and open doors and open doors you go, as my love and faithfulness you sow!

Let Me lighten your load as you go. Let Me open the fields into which you sow. Here we go—"

PURPOSE AND FAITH

"And on this Mount [Zion] shall the Lord of hosts make for all peoples a feast of rich things [symbolic of His coronation festival inaugurating the reign of the Lord on earth, in the wake of a background of gloom, judgment and terror], a feast of wines on the lees—of fat things full of marrow, of wines on the lees well refined" (Isaiah 25:6 AMP).

I have known Rosalie since 1976. Her enthusiasm for the Lord and His Presence is absolutely contagious. One of her most endearing qualities is her desire that all of God's children reach their destiny. Recently, the Lord began to remind her of her own destiny—so today we thought it appropriate to remind you of yours!

Why should we care about what God has in store for us? Because each new day is an adventure in His Kingdom. His joy is our strength, His power goes before and behind us, His Presence comforts us, and His destiny gives our lives purpose. What He does in our lives flows through us and changes the hearts and lives of others—sometimes when we are even unaware of it! They are eternal moments with eternal purpose!

Example: One day it was snowing in northern Idaho, the very first snow of the season. Some viewed this snow with absolute fear because of their "experience" of a year with a record snowfalls. Some viewed the snow with overwhelming joy because they love to ski and play and find adventure in it. As those who know Jesus, we should remember that our experience should be a stepping stone to fresh courage, not to fear.

Is snow difficult to deal with? It can be, if you don't have the right tires or vehicle to get around in it. Like life, if we are not properly prepared for what we face, it can cause us great danger.

Yet Scripture says that God gives the snow from the "Treasury of Heaven for a time of war and trouble." It is supposed to slow us down. It is supposed to give us a quiet peace. It is a gift of such beauty that, when mixed with that sense of hope and faith, makes even the longest of winters beautiful to see. It's all in how we view life itself—from faith or from fear.

Let's all take life as the adventure it was meant to be. The joy of seeing God at the breaking of the dawn or the setting of the sun; the knowledge of His Presence within us, before and behind us like the Pillar of Cloud and the Pillar of Fire; the excitement of knowing that He has chosen us all to be an integral part of His eternal plan—these are the moments to cherish and look forward to each and every morning. Great changes are upon us! Look for them with joy!

Love, Faye

Day Four

"Rejoice in the Lord always [delight, gladden yourselves in Him];
again I say, Rejoice!"
PHILIPPIANS 4:4 AMP

EXCERPT FROM *A WALK WITH JESUS*:

"Pile up My Words in your heart. Make of your heart a storehouse. My Words will guide and comfort you. I am with you, to guide you, moment by moment. Praise Me and rejoice. Rejoice evermore. Everything sifted through a praising heart comes out joy and gladness. Rejoice in everything. Praise Me in all things. I will lead you, my child, gently and with care. Do not ever fret. Patience! It has to be wrought in the Spirit, step by step. Worry not with the minute, but keep your eye on the big picture. What is past, is past. The need is for that which is to come."

CHANGE THE CHANNEL

What kind of movie is playing in your head? Faith is learning to change the channel from fear to faith in every circumstance. If you are like me, sometimes it's hard to do, but God's Word works!

Philippians 4:6-7 is a familiar read:

"Do not fret or have any anxiety about anything, but in every circumstance and in everything, by prayer and petition (definite requests), with thanksgiving, continue to make your wants known to God. And God's peace [shall be yours, that tranquil state of a soul assured of its salvation through Christ, and so fearing nothing from God and being content with its earthly lot of whatever sort that is, that peace] which transcends all understanding, shall garrison and mount guard over your hearts and minds in Christ Jesus" (AMP).

Everyone faces fearful circumstances, whether illness or anything that may seem to destroy our lives. It's what we do with that emotion that will determine whether it overcomes us or we overcome it. When people want to tell us horror stories of any circumstance, we need to put up our hand and remind them that we belong to the Living God and therefore, will be fine whatever the outcome. One of the most difficult trials, for example, is cancer.

I have a dear friend (who actually led my husband to Christ), who had overcome brain cancer seven, yes SEVEN times. They had given her a death sentence so many times. She waved them off and reminded them that only Jesus has the keys to death, hell, and the grave. And she wasn't going there, she was a citizen of Heaven and therefore would go home when He chose and not before. It was an amazing testimony. At age 79, she slogged through mud up to her knees to minister in remote villages in the Philippines. Her faith was determined—and filled with joy no matter what the outcome would be. She went Home to be with the Lord in the late 1990's. But she went home with victory on her lips and joy in her heart!

As one friend often puts it, "What are you going to do, scare me with Heaven?" We are citizens of another country—not of this earth. While we live in the natural realm and must do what has to be done, we also belong to the supernatural realms of the Holy Spirit. Our lives belong to DAD. Jesus gave us access to wonderful places we cannot even comprehend: the very Throne Room of the God of all creation! If the God who created the universe allows us to hang out with Him, how can anything we face on the earth keep us down? We all can change the channel of our brains from the movie of death and destruction to the Holy of Holies. In HIS Presence is fullness of joy.

Rejoice! Rejoice! Rejoice!

Love, Faye

Day Five

"Thy word is true from the beginning:
every one of thy righteous judgments endureth forever."
Psalm 119:160 KJV

Excerpt from *A Walk with Jesus*:

"Ease on down the road. As each sand of the hourglass falls, so shall each step be taken, one by one. It is not the big blast, but the continual pressing in that builds the strong foundation. Be not afraid of the slow start. Rest in my preparations and my love for you. Step by step, day by day, resolve to walk in what I have given you to walk in, and more will be added. Be not pressured nor grieved over lack of action. It is there. It is there. Remain in my peace for you. Do not let oppression knock on your door, for all shall go as I have planned. Remain unmoved by outside pressures. Simply move as I lead, step by step. Remain agile and alert. Be at peace, my child."

Greater Things!

One Sunday I had a vision of an hourglass with only a tiny bit of sand left in the top. It seemed that the Lord was saying that He was about to turn over a new period of time—one in which whatever destiny we have is going to be completed.

When Jesus made the wine at the marriage at Cana, He remarked to His mother, Mary, that "it wasn't His time yet." He had not yet begun His ministry on earth, yet Mary was fully aware of His Divine nature.

All of us are fully aware of the Divine Presence of God within us if we know Him personally. We know that it means we have a purpose and a plan to fulfill. We also have felt at one time or another like we were slogging through quicksand.

One day in 2003, I was sitting at the piano worshiping by myself. Suddenly I had a vision of somewhere in the Middle East. I found myself with a few other people, including a man who was a translator. We ladies were dressed in traditional black Arabic garb. We walked through an open air market, and approached an old woman who was selling sheep. I purchased a tiny black lamb. I carried that lamb to a meeting with a local sheik (a tribal leader). The moment we entered his meeting room, the lamb transformed into a large white dove, flew up to the sheik's shoulder, and landed there. At that moment, the opportunity came to lead him, his family, and guards to Christ. As soon as they had fallen to their knees, our group was whisked away in the Holy Spirit to once again stand in the open air market. The little black lamb reappeared in my arms and we returned it to the woman we bought it from. It all happened without anyone knowing who we were!

What the Lord asked was interesting: "Are you willing to be faceless, unknown, in order to accomplish the 'greater things' spoken of in My Word?"

To see and be a part of those "greater things," then YES!!!!!

God can use us more if we aren't in the way. Jesus made the wine, the very best wine, at the end of the wedding. No one knew who made it, by the way, except Mary and those who gathered the vessels to contain it. WE ALL are the vessels of the very last wine. The very best anointing and the very greatest moves of God are before us. As that hourglass completes this cycle and is turned over to a new day, we are at the beginning of the time of fulfillment. If we are willing to allow Him to do the most powerful works of His plan, we will see and be a part of things as spectacular as translation, salvation, and transformation. All of you are part of that plan and purpose!

We encourage you to find the pathway, see the Lord, and walk forward into that purpose of God. We can hardly wait to see what God has in store for all of us!

Love, Faye

Day Six

"He calls his own sheep by name and leads them out.
After he has gathered his own flock, he walks ahead of them, and
they follow him because they know his voice. They won't follow a
stranger; they will run from him because they don't know his voice."
JOHN 10:3-5 NLT

EXCERPT FROM *A WALK WITH JESUS*:

*"You have learned mighty and glorious truths. Ponder them in your heart.
Delight in them. Digest them further. My sheep shall hear my voice. They shall
hear and rejoice. They shall no longer walk in darkness. They shall see the light
and make their way toward that light. Glory in the highest! My people shall
have ears to hear and eyes to see, and they shall go forth as the mighty army
of the Lord. Break forth in singing, for the time has come to rejoice mightily,
for the Glory of the Lord shall shine upon His people, and they shall not doubt
nor fear, but they shall move out with confidence, knowing that their Lord is
going before them, making straight the path. Glory, hallelujah!"*

KNOWING HIM

When you get to know people, you learn the sound of their voice.
They can call you on the telephone and fail to tell you who they are, and
you still recognize their voice. (Unless you're in an office where everyone ends up copying your tone…then everyone sounds like you.)

When we know God intimately and connect to His heart, then we
hear Him and our lives and those around us are changed forever. His
Glory rises over us in ways we could never have imagined! We can have
the personal confidence to even see the lives of our loved ones changed
as God begins to move. If we know Him, we will hear Him!

Example: When I was growing up, my best friend's name was
Shirley. We did everything together, up until she met her husband and
got married. She and I knew exactly the sound of each other's voices—

and still do today. She moved away from our area and she and her husband bought a sheep ranch. We were both "Christians" because we went to church, but neither of us was aware that God still speaks in a personal way.

As time went on, I came to know the Lord, but Shirley would call me and you could tell she was sad. She listened to me tell her about the things God did for me, but only said she thought I was "centered."

One day, one of Shirley's sheep went into labor. The baby lamb was breached in the mother's birth canal, and the veterinarian was unable to come quickly enough to save it. Shirley reached in, turned the lamb, and helped it come out safely. As the tiny black lamb slid out into her hands, she heard a soft voice say, "I Am the Lamb of God, I was born for you, and I give you life. Just as you gave life to this baby lamb, I give life to you."

Shirley took care of the lamb, and ran into the house to find her old, dust covered Bible. As she read it, tears streamed down her cheeks, and the gospel of Jesus became so clear that it changed her entire life. The soft whisper of the Holy Spirit spoke to her heart. Today we can share more than just old memories, we can share what God is saying and doing in our lives.

The Great Shepherd knows His sheep. He speaks to His sheep. He uses YOU as the soft conduit of His Holy Spirit's Voice. If OUR voice is right, the sound of His Voice comes through! If we are open to listen, quick to obey, joyous to receive, and love to hear Him, there are greater things in store. Rosalie's deepest heart desire is for all to hear the Voice of our wonderful Lord and do what He asks. There are wonders waiting for us that we can't comprehend, and God's Glory is about to be released in new ways. So we encourage you today to listen, trust, hear, and ask for eyes to see it all! And then move out with confidence!

Love, Faye

Day Seven

"You gave abundant showers,
O God; you refreshed your weary inheritance.
Your people settled in it, and from your bounty,
God, you provided for the poor."

PSALM 68:9-10 NIV

EXCERPT FROM *A WALK WITH JESUS*:

"Prepare your heart to receive my goodness and prosperity. Prepare through vigilance, perseverance and dedication to My Word and My Presence. Carry forth My Word to you, prepare and rejoice, for the day draws near when my ways and preparations for you shall be seen."

GOD IS WITH YOU

Over the years, all of us have heard the term "preparation." We have been told to prepare for all the doom and gloom scenarios. We have been told to get out of debt; we have been told to do all sorts of things in "preparation" for what is to come. However, most of us have no way to accomplish the things these would-be prophets tell us to do. This has often made us all concerned about whether we've messed up and whether God would really take care of us in a pinch.

Here is your encouragement for the day: God will never leave you nor forsake you. If you are poor, He will make sure you are fed. If you are broken-hearted, He will heal you and comfort you. If you don't have a safe place to live, He is your strong tower and fortress. Keep Psalm 91 close to your heart. You belong to the King of kings and Lord of lords. Nothing is impossible with the Lord!

The word from *A Walk with Jesus* that you read above explains what is really meant by "preparation." It doesn't mean go build a bunker to hide in. It doesn't mean panic and worry about what is to come. It DOES mean that God has been preparing you already throughout your walk with Him. As you dedicate your heart to be aware, to keep moving forward no matter the circumstance, and to seek the Presence of God, there is nothing that can stand in the way of His Hand in Your life. He will open your understanding to the secrets of His ways. He will accomplish things through you that are mighty!

Love, Faye

"...The people who know their God shall be strong, and carry out great exploits." —Daniel 11:32 NKJV

Day Eight

"The lips of the righteous feed many, but fools die for lack of wisdom.
The blessing of the LORD makes one rich,
and He adds no sorrow with it."
PROVERBS 10:21-22 NKJV

EXCERPT FROM *A WALK WITH JESUS*:

"Step up higher into My Kingdom. Do not be satisfied with yesterday's bless-ings. Appropriate new and more expanded blessings for today and expect even more tomorrow. Step forth over the threshold into a constant state of worship and praise. Keep your eye and your mind and your heart's eye continually on Me. Contain not thy spirit. Let it soar in communion and praise with Me."

THE BRIGHTNESS OF HIS LOVE

You can certainly tell a person who loves the Lord by their counte-nance, and by their love of worship. Blessings seem to follow them wher-ever they go. You can tell someone who loves the Lord by their willingness to laugh—to show forth the joy of the Lord. You can see in them all of the attributes of 1 Corinthians 13 (patience, kindness, not envious, not boastful, not conceited, do not act improperly, not selfish, not provoked, keep no record of wrongs, do not find joy in unrighteous-ness, rejoice in truth, do not worry about people's faults but believe in them no matter what the circumstance).

While we may fail in one or two of these areas on occasion, the majority of these things "ooze" from the Believer who loves and stays in worship to the Lord.

I used to be very intrigued by Rosalie's smile. When I first met her, I simply couldn't believe someone could smile that much—especially since I knew she was going through some difficult times. But that smile, that "rainbow of joy" oozed God's love. It leaked out of her in spite of her circumstances. Ultimately, that's how I came to know Christ person-ally. It was the Sonshine that radiated from someone who loves Him.

That love brought me the greatest blessing of all—friendship with God and with the people of His Kingdom!

All of us should love the Lord so much that the windows of our hearts show His love. We can only do that through relationship—worship and praise and trust. May the Lord reveal to you today how powerful His Presence is in worship. May His blessings overtake you and be poured out over you. May He turn your mourning into joy and your sorrow into dancing. And may every trial show forth the deliverance of your loving Father!

Love, Faye

Day Nine

"I prayed to the LORD, and he answered me. He freed me from all
my fears. Those who look to him for help will be radiant with joy;
no shadow of shame will darken their faces. In my desperation
I prayed, and the LORD listened; he saved me from all my troubles.
For the angel of the LORD is a guard; he surrounds and defends
all who fear him. Taste and see that the LORD is good.
Oh, the joys of those who take refuge in him!"

PSALM 34:4-8 NLT

EXCERPT FROM *WHEN GOD SPEAKS TO MY HEART*:

*"Today is a new day. Your life is being transformed from the dust of shattered
dreams, bringing forth the promises that I have spoken. My hand of mercy is
upon you. All you have experienced shall become the platform upon which you
stand, for you have experienced much and grown tremendously. Take refuge in
the knowledge that I have a plan for your life. Struggle not with the details, but
look to Me. All will come about naturally and be a joy to your heart. Proclaim
my goodness, and together we shall see victory!"*

HOPE

No matter what country, background, or ethnicity we may have, all
of us have experienced disappointment in our lives. Whether it is a
desire to serve the Lord in ministry, or a plan to expand a business, or
the hope of the bride in her new marriage, things don't always turn out
as we had hoped. These are times of "shattered dreams."

There was a time in both Rosalie's and my own life where it seemed
as if everything kept derailing—no forward momentum but lots of backwards falling. "Hope deferred makes the heart sick..." is the way
Scripture puts it (Proverbs 13:12 NKJV). Yet we learned to move
forward and not give up, in spite of heartaches and what seemed like
failures. We learned that friendships are huge helps in times of trouble,

as are our deepening relationships with the Lord. And we learned that what we THINK we see, may not be what God is doing!

And there is good news! The second part of Proverbs 13:12 which we rarely hear says, "...but when the desire comes, it is a tree of life." God is all about life. The reason Jesus went to the cross is to allow us access to life—both here on earth and throughout eternity (John 3:16). When God created the earth and all that is in it, He commanded all of it to prosper and bring forth life. He asks us to be the vessels of His "River of Life," the Holy Spirit. He doesn't break "bruised reeds," people who are sad and hurting. He came to bring us LIFE and that MORE ABUNDANTLY (John 10:10).

When it seems like there is no hope, there is God who creates the dawn. When the dreams appear to be dead, there is the God of resurrection! Tomorrow is a new day for us all. What happens today may be the stepping stone to breakthrough you have waited for. Faith is built on what we can't see, but we know God has in store for us. May the fulfilled desires of your heart come quickly, and may all that delays your hope be destroyed by the blessings and love of our Savior!

Love, Faye

Day Ten

"So it shall be, while My glory passes by, that I will put you in the cleft of the rock, and will cover you with My hand while I pass by."

EXODUS 33:22 NKJV

EXCERPT FROM *WHEN GOD SPEAKS TO MY HEART*:

"Relax in My Presence and lift up your heart to Me with steadfast love and adoration. Let Me be your place of habitation, just as you are Mine. I am your steadfast Rock of protection. There is a cleft in that Rock for you. Nestle into that cleft with trust and love, as a child snuggles into his parent's lap for warmth and affirmation. I long to be that quiet place of rest and affirmation for you. Rest in Me, child. Rest in Me. When you have rested and learned of that quietness in Me, then we can proudly step out together in service and in love. Learn of my love for you, child. Rely on and receive deeper levels of that love. It is yours. Receive, and then become a restorer, an instrument for restoring that love to the brethren. It is yours, my child. Reach out and receive it."

GRACE, PEACE, TO YOU BE MULTIPLIED

Jesus came as a Restorer of the breach. In other words, He not only restored the relationship of God to His beloved people, but He came to restore all of the things in our lives. As His ambassadors, that's now our job too! Trouble is, sometimes we're not very good at it. The good news is, no matter what people say to us, God is the One with the final say! There really IS a place in the "cleft of the Rock" where we are redeemed and kept safe.

One day I mentioned to a family member (who is a Spirit-filled Christian) that we needed prayer for God to help us with our finances. She looked at me with disdain and said, "God's not going to help you with that, you got yourself into the problem, you'll have to get yourself out." With that, she turned and walked away. My heart was crushed!

I went immediately to the Word to see what the true story was, and found that God is our Redeemer, not our condemnation. He is fully aware that we have weaknesses and faults, yet His love for us reaches into the depths and pulls us out giving us newfound wisdom and grace. This doesn't mean we can willfully sin against Him, but it does mean that when circumstances are out of our control, He hears our cries and answers!

Here is just a sampling of the Scriptures God gave me. I pray they will encourage your heart to know that no matter what you are experiencing, God has a plan to restore your life!

Hebrews 4:16 NKJV: "Let us therefore come boldly to the throne of grace, that we may obtain mercy and find grace to help in time of need."

Psalm 136:23-24 NKJV: "Who remembered us in our lowly state, for His mercy endures forever; and rescued us from our enemies, for His mercy endures forever."

Psalm 130:7 NKJV: "O Israel, hope in the LORD; for with the LORD there is mercy, and with Him is abundant redemption."

Psalm 40:2-3 NKJV: "He also brought me up out of a horrible pit, out of the miry clay, and set my feet upon a rock and established my steps. He has put a new song in my mouth — praise to our God; many will see it and fear, and will trust in the LORD."

John 14:14 NKJV: "If you ask anything in My name, I will do it."

Psalm 103:13-14 NKJV: "As a father pities his children, so the LORD pities those who fear Him. For He knows our frame, He remembers that we are dust."

The word "pities" in that passage is the Hebrew word *racham*. It means to soothe, to cherish, to love deeply, to have compassion, to be tender, to demonstrate mercy…you get the picture. For those who love God and are called according to His purpose, everything works together for good. We are not lost, and we will not be ashamed. You are the head and not the tail. God loves you and will help in His grace and mercy no matter what you are facing!

It is our heart that you will experience the grace and mercy of our Lord in every circumstance. We pray that condemnation will be far from you, that you will find rest and love in His Presence, safe from negative words. May restoration come to your life in every area!

Love, Faye

"…Without faith it is impossible to please Him, for he who comes to God must believe that He is, and that He is a rewarder of those who diligently seek Him." —Hebrews 11:6 NKJV

Day Eleven

"So shall they fear the name of the LORD from the west, and his glory
from the rising of the sun. When the enemy shall come in like
a flood, the Spirit of the LORD shall lift up a standard against him."

ISAIAH 59:19 KJV

EXCERPT FROM *WHEN GOD SPEAKS TO MY HEART*:

*"I charge you this day to know the hearts of those around you. Be sincere and
seek to know and love them for who they are. That expression of love will free
their lives from fear and doubt. My love will set them free. Be a messenger of
my love, joy, freedom, and truth. Restore confidence through Me. Help others
see the potential of their lives in Me. Be a standard of love, freedom, and joy.
Every time you hug each one and smile at each one, you impart these precious
elements of my heart. It is all part of my plan.*

"Love as I love you!"

THE STANDARD BEARERS

We are called to be the standard bearers of God's love to a world
filled with trials, brokenness, and hard places. And if you think about it,
ALL Christians are called to the same. We are to be the ones who allow
the River of Life to splash all over anyone and everyone we meet!

When we met Jesus, His love touched our broken hearts and gave
us a whole new outlook on life. That personal encounter deeply changed
us. He didn't use His rod to beat us up that day, or tell us what losers we
were; He simply reached out and gave us a giant spiritual hug. And our
lives were transformed by love. I will never forget the sight of a golden
light washing through my living room, a dog that got scared and ran to
the corner, and the gentle whisper of God's voice that said, "I love you;
there is room in My plan for you"—all because Rosalie took the time to
stop by my house when I was an unbeliever. She was a standard-bearer
of love.

We hope and pray that you will all take this opportunity to give those around you such a hug. Life is difficult; things are in the red zone of danger around us. Our lives hang in the balance daily—everyone desperately needs peace and love to help them make it. Be attentive, and be the standard-bearer of Christ. You can make eternal history!

Love, Faye

Day Twelve

"Love is patient and kind. Love is not jealous or boastful or proud or rude. It does not demand its own way. It is not irritable, and it keeps no record of being wronged. It does not rejoice about injustice but rejoices whenever the truth wins out. Love never gives up, never loses faith, is always hopeful, and endures through every circumstance."

1 CORINTHIANS 13:4-7 NLT

EXCERPT FROM *WHEN GOD SPEAKS TO MY HEART*:

"My Child, there are all kinds of love. Love that rejoices in the accomplishments of others, love that sticks close through failure and pain, love that lifts the burden of wrongs endured, and love that persists against all odds. My Word spoken compassionately and then believed and received in the heart—this is the love I have provided you to give. Don't let up when the odds seem slim and defeat wants to prevail. Turn defeat into victory by claiming My Word and standing on that truth, undaunted by the passing scene, for My Word stands and my promises are sure. Remain strong in your faith and strong in the love I have given you. Then give that love to others. Be a giver, not a taker. Offer your love to others without thought of return, taking only from Me, my love, and you will never lack. I love you."

WHERE IS YOUR HEART?

Have you ever been right AND wrong at the same time? Can you speak truth wrongly? You betcha. Love is a heart condition, and sometimes we don't see real truth inside ourselves. Sometimes we help ourselves into relationship messes without even trying.

I used to work for a police agency. In that job, accuracy was of paramount importance. If a report was inaccurate or missing some parts, criminals could be let out on the street after an arrest. After spending most of my adult life checking paperwork and reports every single morning, I became somewhat forceful in my approach to getting the paperwork corrected. A small number of the officers labeled me

"Colonel" behind my back, and sometimes even a few less polite terms. While I truly loved each of these officers and respected their jobs, often I would be harsh in my requests for amendments to their work. Why? Because I had some pride seeds in my heart instead of love! My approach often made them enraged.

When it was time for me to retire after more than 31 years on the job, a small handful of the officers let out that pent-up rage. Some of those final confrontations were extremely hurtful. I realized the treatment I was receiving was my own fault for the methods I had employed over the years. The things I asked the officers to do were RIGHT, but the WAY I asked was often WRONG, and very harmful to the working relationships.

Whether it is a family relationship, the family of God, or a working relationship, it is always easy to take a wrong turn when we have a seed of pride instead of a garden of love. The Scripture verse today and Rosalie's book excerpt, remind us all that love isn't about being RIGHT, it's about sharing the heart of God in any situation. Truth is very important, but truth must come from a heart of love, not judgment or pride. Jesus didn't come to judge the world, He came to save it (John 3:17). As His servants, that's our job too.

We would like to encourage all of us to take a heart-check. The Bible admonishes us to keep a watch on our hearts, for out of it flow the issues of life (Proverbs 4:23). At this most stressful time in history, when money is tight, relatives are around, and the "to-do" list is long and arduous, a quick heart-check is good to keep us from adding to our own stressful situations. God does not want you to navel-watch or self condemn, He just wants you to be aware and let Him have everything immediately. He gives us freedom, joy, peace, hope, and He always sees the best in us. We pray that all of us will be lovers of mankind; gardens of love brimming with the joy of the Holy Spirit!

Love, Faye

"When people's lives please the LORD; even their enemies are at peace with them." —Proverbs 16:7 NLT

Day Thirteen

"So humble yourselves before God. Resist the devil and he will flee from you. Come close to God, and God will come close to you."

JAMES 4:7-8 NLT

EXCERPT FROM *A WALK WITH JESUS*:

"What is the difference between intensity and being tense and over-anxious? Intensity is pressing in, knowing that I will bring to pass that which you are contending for, that I will bring to pass that which you are pressing in for. Being over-anxious and being tense is synonymous with doubt. It is trying to twist my arm by doing all the right things to get Me to bring it about. Be not tense. Be not over-anxious, but stand still, intently still, with perseverance of spirit, with rejoicing and thanksgiving, stopping the enemy at every turn, allowing no infractions. See the salvation of your Lord. I am fighting for you, and ours is the victory."

ENEMIES AND VICTORIES

Sometimes in our lives it feels like the enemy gets pretty riled up. That is especially true with people who walk closely in personal fellowship with the Lord. The devil flat doesn't like it and wants to wreck us up. Gee, isn't that just too bad if he doesn't like it. So, if he gets riled up, just stomp him or his buddies like the cockroaches that they are. The Word says we are to resist the devil and he will flee from us. The excerpt from Rosalie's book reminds us not to get all worked up, but to stand fast and know that God is fighting for us. So what does that mean?

Once I received a frantic call from someone who told me that the enemy was trying to ruin their meeting. The people were very upset because they sensed a demonic presence. My answer? "So what? Boot him out—he's not invited!" We carry the Living God within us. No one can stand against Him. We don't have to be worried, fearful, or tense, because the God Who created the entire universe is OUR DAD, OUR LORD, OUR FRIEND!

It works the same with things we are praying for. If we get tense (and believe me, I can be as tense as anyone—grinding my teeth tense, in fact), then we live in a place of fear and worry instead of faith. And the enemy loves it. He can whisper in our ear all sorts of things when there is fear or anxiety. "You're not going to make it." "You're a failure, nobody wants you around." "You will lose everything." "You can't have THAT, you are not worthy, God won't answer you." Yada, yada, yada, blah, blah, blah. So how do you resist all that hogwash?

A pastor friend once told me that when the negative voices get cranked, go make a peanut butter sandwich. (OK, I admit it; I'd rather have chocolate.) The fact is, it works. Resist the devil. Laugh. Sing praises, stand firm on what the Word says, not what nastiness is coming at you. The Word says that the promises of God are "Yea and amen." That means whatever you pray for in His name is yours.

But, but, but. No buts. You are beloved; you are adopted into the Family of the Living God. You are part of His Body. You are one with the Savior of all mankind. So relax. Open your mouth, let out all the tension, shout to the Lord in triumph, and receive His promises!

Love, Faye

Day Fourteen

"Therefore I, a prisoner for serving the Lord, beg you to lead a life worthy of your calling, for you have been called by God. Always be humble and gentle. Be patient with each other, making allowance for each other's faults because of your love. Make every effort to keep yourselves united in the Spirit, binding yourselves together in peace."

EPHESIANS 4:1-3 NLT

EXCERPT FROM *WALKING ON WITH JESUS*:

"I have surrounded you with prayer and love. When one strikes out who feels neither, respond with compassion, for my truth will win out and my compassion shall rule and bind up hurts and fears. Reach out unafraid of repercussions. Reach out and love and let Me take care of the results. Proceed with caution, but proceed with love and acceptance for the one who feels none. I am with you, my child, to bring healing and wholeness. Let Me lead, and together we shall see miracles abounding, love and joy surrounding your life at every turn."

THE RESPONSE FROM GOD'S HEART

Today's word from Rosalie's book is a tough one for all of us. People who strike at us usually do it because they feel neither love, nor God's favor. Our response can bring life or death. If we snarl back, it means that we've forgotten that God fights for us in all situations!

Several years ago, I went on a mission trip with a team from several churches. No one knew me well, so they assigned me to pray for the church team in charge and gave strict instructions that I was not to do anything else. After the first week of intense traveling from place to place, we returned to the capital city for the final week of services. I was somewhat disappointed that I had not been allowed to participate in anything, but I simply placed my disappointment in the hands of the Lord and refused to whine to the leadership about it.

When it came time for the meetings, one of the local pastors asked me to play the keyboard. They placed me on the stage and started tuning up their instruments. Then the team leader became angry and refused to let me play. After walking back and forth from my seat several times, the local pastors dragged me back up to the stage and warned the team leader to lay off. (I sort of felt like a ping-pong ball at that point.) I could sense fear in our team leader for my safety, but I kept my big mouth shut on all counts. By the end of the trip, I had not only played the keyboard, but was allowed to pray for people, got a bird's-eye view of all the miracles and healings, and received a gift blessing from the locals. God showed up and released me to participate all on His own, and I didn't have to say a thing!

Disappointment with people comes to all of us, whether it's a pastor who isn't fond of us or our gifts, or a brother or sister who might be insensitive or have another agenda. We live in the earth; we will encounter those sorts of issues all the time. Our response must first be to the Lord—if our hearts hurt, we need to tell Him and ask for a gift of forgiveness, mercy, and grace. I don't know about you, but sometimes I muff it, especially if they make me mad. If we remember Who lives in us, it will be easier and easier to let Him run the encounters in our lives.

We encourage you to follow God in spite of the blocks you may encounter from people who do not understand your calling. God understands and surrounds you with His love and the prayers of the saints. Trust Him to vindicate, protect, and fulfill all that He has promised!

Love, Faye

Day Fifteen

"We shall be satisfied with the goodness of Your house,
of Your holy temple. By awesome deeds in righteousness
You will answer us, O God of our salvation. You who are the
confidence of all the ends of the earth, and of the far-off seas."

PSALM 65:4-5 NKJV

EXCERPT FROM *WHEN GOD SPEAKS TO MY HEART*:

*"Be satisfied with who you are, where you are, and where you are going,
knowing that I hold all things in my hands. Your growth is in my hands, and all
it requires is a willing and dedicated heart, walking with trust, motivated by a
desire to walk in righteousness. Fulfillment and trust walk hand in hand. Trust
in my mighty hand to move on your behalf. Have faith. Trust Me, my child!"*

THE GOODNESS OF THE HOUSE OF THE LORD

What in the world does it mean to be "satisfied" with the "goodness
of the house of the Lord?" We all live in a world where we need help at
every turn, from just paying the bills to dealing with people. So if you're
feeling a little guilty that you need things and more than just
worship...let's set the record straight.

The most important thing we all need is TRUST. Yikes! When bill
collectors are calling every few minutes, and the phone company is
threatening to turn off your service, your second cousin's wife's son has
been breaking into your house and stealing you blind, the news on television is all about doom, despair, and misery, and that woman from
church keeps stopping by to jabber for an hour at a time about how
awful her life is...HELP! How do we turn on the trust-God-meter?
Wear ear plugs?

Personally, the only thing I can do is what King David did: I encourage myself in the Lord. When David was surrounded by threats of death
by stoning (1 Samuel 30:6), he didn't have a Bible. He had remembrance
of what God did that was passed down from his ancestors. There were

some writings, of course, but there was no Bible Bookstore on the corner by the palace. He didn't have the parchments stuffed under his pillow at night. So he only had a personal relationship with God to work with. And that relationship satisfied him, so God called him a "man after His own heart." Trust is built when we run to DAD for absolutely everything!

Several years ago I thought I had lost a very close friend from one of those enemy-inspired conflicts that happen from time to time. We parted under VERY bad circumstances. My heart was crushed and I couldn't do anything but weep. So I really got down and talked to the Lord (through the stuffy nose and swollen eyes) about my grief. Soft peace surrounded me so that I was finally able to get to sleep. The next morning, a prophet friend from the midwest sent me a personal email that told me God was listening and would handle the problem. The man had no knowledge of the incident that had occurred. Within two months, the situation was healed, fixed, repented of, and my friend was back! I was "satisfied" in the goodness of the house of the Lord—in His Holy Spirit, in His love that fulfilled my heart cries.

To be "satisfied" is to be content. God loves it when we run to Him. He longs to be the One Who heals, lifts, touches, gives, changes. Our needs and wants, our desires and hopes are satisfied by His promise of fulfillment. His Presence, His love, His promises satisfy our hearts. If you have great needs today, if you are facing upheaval on every side, run to the Lord Who loves you and be satisfied by the goodness in the House of the Lord.

Love, Faye

Day Sixteen

"How precious is your unfailing love, O God! All humanity finds shelter in the shadow of your wings. You feed them from the abundance of your own house, letting them drink from your river of delights. For you are the fountain of life, the light by which we see."

PSALM 36:7-9 NLT

EXCERPT FROM *WHEN GOD SPEAKS TO MY HEART*:

"Let your life be a bright light. Let your life shine brilliantly that all may see its radiance and warming glow, for My Glory is in you. Let it shine forth unhindered by the daily circumstances beyond your control. Let My Spirit of light and truth govern you, not the situations that would distract you. Walk with determination and choose to bless and bring forth the best in others with graciousness. All of Heaven proclaims My Glory, and this Glory will bless others as you allow my peace, love, and contentment to flow through you. You are blessed."

THE GLOW OF WARMTH

Brrrrr, it's cold outside! Winters in north Idaho can be extremely cold—cold enough that even dogs with heavy fur should be inside at night. I don't know about you, but it feels that way in the earth right now too. No, I'm not talking about "global cooling," but the ice-cold blast of hatred, fear, and sin all around us. It makes the world inhospitable toward our Beloved Lord and all that He stands for! Brrrrr!

Ski lodges are representative of a place of refuge, a place where you can get warmed up in spite of the cold winter outside. WE are called to be a type of "ski lodge" as God's Ambassadors, to show people His warmth and light in the midst of a cold, dark world. When we are walking as His Glory, not our own, we give off a warm "glow." When we are trusting in Christ, we are approachable, beckoning, kind, and loving. Our hearts also get more tender with every passing trial, which is the opposite of worldly people.

Have you ever been around someone who was so needy that everyone runs away when they come in the room? "Uh, I gotta go now." They arrive and people scatter out the door. We must love those people. But to those folks who make everyone scatter, please remember: We are not called to make everyone uncomfortable with our problems. We are called to be confident in the Lord, no matter what we are going through. We are called to GIVE God's love and warmth, not take it from those around us. We are called to be fearless, not fearful. It doesn't mean that we don't ask for prayer, but HOW we do that can mean the difference between bringing people to the light of God or dragging a big black blanket around that covers His light. Desperation scares people away, love draws people to us.

As a former supervisor, I had to learn quickly that being approachable meant listening, and hearing the person's heart. It also meant that my own problems had to be tempered with wisdom and faith, or I could make everyone in the office to have a rotten day. God is our refuge and strength, and we can take His peace, His joy, His love, and His Glory to people in our lives. Let's stand for love—to love one another and to give that love to whoever we meet. That love becomes a warm, inviting light of God to bring souls God's peace and hope amidst a frigid world. God is the God of refreshing, of peace, of redemption, of warmth: a fountain of life!

Love, Faye

Day Seventeen

"Those who obey him will not be punished. Those who are wise will find a time and a way to do what is right, for there is time and a way for everything, even when a person is in trouble."

ECCLESIASTES 8:5-6 NLT

EXCERPT FROM *WALKING ON WITH JESUS*:

"Lightning strikes where it may, and many of my servants shall receive lightning bolts of My Spirit to bring them forth in these last days. Know that you will not be left behind. The past, present, and future blend together to bring forth my perfect will and the beauty of my creative power in your life. You have stood at the door and knocked, and I say to you, 'Enter in and taste of the banquet set for you that you might go out singing, rejoicing, and giving forth of the abundance of my love.' Peace leads the way, love makes a way, and joy secures the way!"

DESTINY

When A Company of Women was formed, God spoke to Rosalie about those who had failed to step into their destiny. Sometimes that happens out of fear, sometimes circumstances overwhelm us. But God is in the business of restoration, redemption, and accomplishment of His plan!

If you have asked, He will answer!

What does that entail? Most of the Christians we know want to be ministers of God—they want to see miracles, participate in healings, save souls, etc. It is a worthy desire, but how do we get there? Sometimes a huge chunk of flesh gets in the middle of that desire. Today's Christianity often contains greed, selfish ambition, and the desire to be seen of men and receive their accolades (and money…). Not the best attitude for a servant.

Jesus said that the Holy Spirit is like the wind—He goes where He wants to and we can't see where He goes (John 3:8). First Corinthians 12 talks about God giving His gifts where HE wants to, based upon His purpose and plan. HE decides who gets what and why. Sometimes, we want to own the gift instead of seek the Giver. That's like trying to own the lightning or the wind—it's not going to happen.

God is about to strike His "ordinary" followers with the lightning of His power, but this is not for us, it's for others. We are living in a time of "gross darkness" according to Isaiah 60, and His Glory is being revealed through us. Prophetically, I'm saying that to be one of God's "lightning rods," we will need to be vigilant. The time for seeking a big name is past. The time for seeking God is upon us. The time for standing together in relationship and friendship is NOW. Our destiny will be fulfilled as long as we remain humble seekers of the Living God, loving Him, and loving one another—we can even make mistakes and God will redeem us, if our hearts are humble before Him.

You were born for such a time as this. The reason you are here is to fulfill a destiny planned for you before the foundation of the world. Don't let it be laid down, fight for it. We will fight for you as well. Don't let worldly ways or what you see or think you know stop you from the pathways of God—be open to His lightning strike when it comes. We are excited to see you shine with the power of the Living God!

Love, Faye

Day Eighteen

"If you abide in Me, and My words abide in you, you will ask what you desire, and it shall be done for you. By this My Father is glorified, that you bear much fruit; so you will be My disciples. As the Father loved Me, I also have loved you; abide in My love."

JOHN 15:7-9 NKJV

EXCERPT FROM *A WALK WITH JESUS*:

"Blessed assurance is yours that the victory is complete. The final countdown has begun and the road is paved with the precious jewels of my constant and abiding love towards you. Relentless and constant has been your desire to please Me, and constant and relentless shall be my hand to you on your behalf. The thorn has been rent from your side, never again to return to plague you. You shall respect yourself, and you shall be respected. Go forth now with assurance and boldness, to walk tall in My Spirit, bearing My Banner of truth and righteousness over thee and thine. Rejoice, my child! The time has come forth for rejoicing. Sing and rejoice, for I have all done things well. Hallelujah!"

THE FAMILY OF GOD

If you love Jesus, and have accepted Him as Lord and Savior, then you are "family." When the people of Israel were told to gather in family groups at the Passover, even those who had no lamb for sacrifice were to be welcomed at their neighbor's family under the covering of blood. If you love Jesus, then you are part of His family, covered by His Blood from death. So regardless of your background, if you have accepted Jesus as Lord, you are "family."

As part of that family, you are deserving of respect, honor, and love. Only in that way can we really lift one another up and encourage each other toward God's plan. Only with that kind of honor and love can we encourage one another when we are struggling in a trial. God is the giver of victory: Jesus' name means "Savior."

This morning we received a phone call about someone who was suffering from a terminal illness who had been asked by several people "when was she going to die." My heart shuddered in grief. Such lack of respect and compassion should not pass the lips of family members. Those words left an echo in the woman's heart—an echo of hopelessness.

Sometimes it is hard to know what to say to someone who is suffering, or who has had a terrible tragedy in their lives. But life and death are in the power of our tongues. God does ALL things well—sometimes we forget. The words we speak to others will echo in their minds, so compassion should be the focus we give them rather than judgment or fear or harshness. God gives the gift of life to us to operate through us. Let me repeat that: God gives the gift of life to us to operate through us!

Like the grapes that ripen to make new wine, anointing gives the power to break chains. Victory belongs to God's family, no matter what the circumstance! We should always send forth that life-giving victory to anyone who is struggling. God loves us, and His tender touch is understanding, kind, patient, and gentle. If you are part of His Family, you are guaranteed the victory, you are promised great and mighty help no matter what problem may come. Rejoice! Share that rejoicing with others! Show everyone that our God is Love!

Love, Faye

Day Nineteen

"Delight yourself also in the LORD, and He shall give you
the desires of your heart. Commit your way to the LORD,
trust also in Him, and He shall bring it to pass. He shall bring forth
your righteousness as the light, and your justice as the noonday.
Rest in the LORD, and wait patiently for Him."

PSALM 37:4-7 NKJV

EXCERPT FROM *A WALK WITH JESUS*:

"It is time. The time is here to know that for which you have been painstakingly prepared. Buckle on your breastplate of peace, brought forth through My Word to you. Within my will for you is found that which shall delight your heart and cause you to rise up and bless My Name. Watch for it. Watch for the fulfillment of your dream to come forth, to bring to birth. Many times you have looked forward to see the fulfillment of your dream. Now, you shall see it in the now. Receive unto your heart the fulfillment of the promise. Watch with anticipation, for unto you have I given the desires of your heart. It has been proclaimed! So shall it come forth!"

MOVING FORWARD

If I want to hang out in a peaceful, quiet place, I can get up before dawn, leash up the dog, and head out to Lofts Bay in north Idaho. It is situated toward the rising sun. On days when the sun shines, I know that beauty will greet me at the dawning of the day. And sometimes a beaver and several kinds of waterfowl greet me too! It is a place of peace, a place where the promise of a new day reminds me of God's promises, and where my faith is encouraged.

How do you encourage yourself in the Lord? Everyone has something different that works for them. Sometimes it seems as if our dreams and hopes will never come to pass. We fight a long battle with the forces that want to abort our destinies. (Note: The spirit of abortion is loose in

America as well as in many other places. But YOU belong to the Living God and no spirit can keep you from the love of God. Romans 8:38.)

When fears try to take control, it's time to change the prayer. I spoke to a friend the other day who discovered that whenever he was becoming fearful or frustrated over an issue, praying for others who are suffering the same problem changed his faith to overcoming faith. THAT's learning how to encourage yourself in the Lord!

It's like a football game or a war. We can't win if we're always on the defense. We have to take ground. We have to have a good OFFENSE. If all we ever do is stand in the huddle and cry out for help but never take the offense, we cannot win. We have to move forward!

Over the years, there have been trying times where I have felt "locked" into desperation crying for help. My prayers over the situation became unproductive, because all I could do was beg the Lord for help. Faith says that God's promises are yea and amen, but fear causes desperation. God says in His Word to come BOLDLY before the throne of grace, not as a beggar, but as a child of the Living God.

If you are there in a situation in your life, grab the Sword of the Lord, strap on that breastplate, put on the helmet, and stand with patience in the faith that God gives each of us. Encourage yourself with peace—believing the Word of the Lord over your life. As it says in the word from Rosalie's book, "it is time." We can trust Him to complete the plan.

Love, Faye

Day Twenty

"But all who listen to me will live in peace,
untroubled by fear of harm."

PROVERBS 1:33 NLT

EXCERPT FROM *A WALK WITH JESUS*:

"Teach your heart to listen with greater confidence. My Word to you is made known in my little ways. Prepare your heart to listen with ever-increasing adeptness. My Word to you is clear and straightforward. Meaningful words of love and guidance pour forth from Me to you. Let your heart be alert and ready, assured and at peace in the presence of My Heart. Your ways are in Me, and you shall not trip. Steady on, my child, with renewed confidence and vigor. Let your light shine with new radiance of my love. Singleness of mind and heart brings victory. Our days shall follow one upon the other with ever-increasing meaning and speed. Be prepared to move out, and be prepared to love and move in my love for you."

GO, GO, GO

One of the most common words in the Bible is the shortest word… "go." There are over 1000 references to that word in varying forms throughout the Bible. So when God says to be prepared to "move out" or "go," He means it!

A nice easy example: One day I distinctly heard the Lord tell me to go buy Rosalie some flowers. Now, that was expensive, and I was not certain I heard correctly. But it sounded like a fun thing to do, so I called the floral shop beside her bookstore and bought a bouquet. On my lunch hour, I stopped in to see if she liked them, and she told me that it was the anniversary of her opening the store! The gift of those flowers meant a great deal to her. I was clueless, but God was not. He is aware of every small detail of your life.

Another friend of mine was specifically told to go forward in church and tell a woman who was crying that she was praying for her. She gave her name and told her the message. After the service, she learned that the woman's child had recently died...and the daughter's name was the same as hers. The gentleness of God's heart touched the woman's brokenness and gave her a tiny moment of peace. She saw it as a message from God that He was thinking of her.

Be confident of the Lord in your heart, of His Voice in your spirit. Trust His love to bring joy to others through you. As the world gets darker and more difficult for all, God's love and voice in you and through you will be a lifeline, and will change the lives of many. As you trust and believe, more "crazy spiritual things" will happen to you—and that still small, voice of the Holy Spirit will lead you onward. So move out with confidence!

Love, Faye

Day Twenty-one

"…Keeping our eyes on Jesus, the champion who initiates
and perfects our faith. Because of the joy awaiting him,
he endured the cross, disregarding its shame.
Now he is seated in the place of honor beside God's throne."

HEBREWS 12:2 NLT

EXCERPT FROM *WALKING ON WITH JESUS*:

"Believe this day all that I have lain before you to do and to be. Your work has been given to you to do by Me, and I shall carry it through to the very end, every last jot and tittle. Release unto Me your fears for today and tomorrow. Nothing shall befall you that we cannot handle together for good, to the praising, joyful, trusting spirit. Rejoice this day and be glad, for the foundation has been laid with soundness, and the structure of my love has been built exceedingly well."

IMPACT THE WORLD

The word out of Rosalie's book for today gives us several hints at how to impact our world for Christ:

1) Believe.

2) Release your fears.

3) Rejoice.

Many years ago, I was insecure. To be honest, that insecurity kept me from moving into any kind of destiny. I spent most of my time looking at my circumstances instead of walking forward. My parents had divorced several times while I was growing up, and my first marriage collapsed when I met Jesus. I felt rejected, abandoned, and ashamed. After the divorce, I noticed that I wanted to attach my heart to anyone who paid any attention to me. That was God—I asked Him to let me know Him first, and then let the "right one" come later. Was this easy? No. It was very difficult, as the loneliness seemed most poignant at Christmastime and other holidays.

During this time, my beloved church at the time broke up, my mother died, and my workplace seemed to blow up with gossip and back-biting. It was an all-out assault on my ability to handle life. I begged the Lord to get me out of there and set me free. He didn't. Through it all, God helped me lean on Him and start believing His Word. I literally lived in the Bible. If you were to look at that particular Book today, you would find highlights, circles, dates, arrows, all sorts of things that God spoke to my heart during that time.

Ten-plus years afterward, in 1989, a wonderful man came into my life. He fell flat on his face in love with me. His gentle love slowly healed my heart from rejection, and now, more than 20 years later, we still have an excellent marriage. But it took 10 years of struggle to get my own heart away from co-dependence or foolish expectations that only end in disaster. I learned that God is Who He says He is—my Friend, my Provider, my Savior.

GOD is our source, not our circumstances. GOD is our life, not our spouse. GOD provides and His Presence, which is what we should dwell in. He will not fail us, and He longs for us to believe His Word. He longs for us to dump our fears and know in our hearts that He will get us where we are supposed to be. And He longs for us to experience the joy of His Kingdom. After all, He gave His life for that resurrection Glory in your life!

Love, Faye

Day Twenty-two

"You have also given me the shield of Your salvation;
Your right hand has held me up, Your gentleness has made me great.
You enlarged my path under me; so that my feet did not slip."
PSALM 18:35-36 NKJV

EXCERPT FROM *WALKING ON WITH JESUS*:

"Strength, I have promised strength to your body, soul, and spirit. Step up higher in the knowledge of my love. Step up higher in the abundance of My Spirit of Grace. You have longed to see my face. It is reflected in My Grace. It is a place reserved for you. In the mist of clamor and din is my peace, a place reserved to walk in and together, we'll find a steady peace of mind that transcends every hindrance conceived. It is yours because you have believed. There is a place where My Spirit of Grace breaks down all the barriers to the soul. It is found with a price, not a life that seems nice, but one fought on the battlefield for gain, the battle for freedom and life. It's a battle that must be fought, for it is there that victories of spirit, body, and soul are wrought, the goal, that you might be whole."

GRACE — MY FAVORITE GIFT

The word "grace" in the Bible means unmerited favor. Heavy emphasis on the "unmerited" part. Simply put, it means none of us can work it up, make it perfect on our own, or achieve God's love by what we do. In short, God simply loves us because He loves us. If you think about it, that is amazing — considering He's the Guy Who created the universe.

The battles we must fight are real. They range in everything from finances to relationships, physical to spiritual. All of this requires faith, but in all of it, there is God's wonderful, awesome grace.

My husband and I used to live in a less than 900-square-foot home that had no kitchen cabinets, no closets, and no light fixtures (only bare light bulbs hanging by a wire). The basement was always damp, as it was made of stones that leaked water in wet weather. The house had lots of mice. We had a very large Newfoundland dog and no fence. Myron's teenage son lived with us off and on, which made us pretty cramped for space. The previous tenant was a smoker, so the vague smell of cigarettes permeated the paint on the walls. We both had very stressful jobs, and very little income. Myron was working graveyard shift at a mental health facility. Both of us nearly went crazy in the confined space and hectic schedule.

One day, I cracked around the edges and starting swearing at the Lord. Yes, I lost it. I threw one whale of a temper tantrum to my Savior. After my tirade, the phone rang and I was invited to a meeting with a minister at a friend's home that night. I needed to get away, so I went.

The minute I walked in the door, before any introductions, the minister walked up to me, stuck out his hand to shake mine, and said, "The Lord says to you, you don't have to talk to Me that way."

Wow. That took me aback. I was embarrassed, but mostly blessed that the Lord had heard me. I didn't have the tantrum to a God who wasn't listening. He heard every bad word. I was excited. Within a few months, He made a way for us to obtain a real house with cabinets and real light fixtures. His love endures forever. His gentleness brought life back to my heart.

Our God is gentle, and He loves us more than life itself. He hears every word we speak or think, and we should be very grateful. I love Him because He hears me, even when I'm not in the best of moods. He hears me when I'm broken and weeping. He hears me when I'm angry. He doesn't turn me away when I can't handle a situation; He covers me with His Grace and gives me His strength. And that gives me great joy.

Today, God wants you to know that His gentleness will make you great. His salvation is sure, His love is forever, and He will never fail you, no matter how badly you may fail Him. He is eternal, and He showers us with strength and grace in everything we face. He loves you!

Love, Faye

Day Twenty-three

"You shall love the LORD your God with all your heart, with all your soul, and with all your mind. This is the first and great commandment. And the second is like it: You shall love your neighbor as yourself. On these two commandments hang all the Law and the Prophets."

MATTHEW 22:37-40 NKJV

EXCERPT FROM *THE SINGING BRIDE*:

"Mighty plans I have for thee. Blessings from sea to bright shining sea. Be that beacon light for all to see, as from the enemy they flee. A place of refuge from the storm. A place to regroup and become warm. To seek my face in brand new ways. Tattered and torn, tired and worn, my troops shall come to thee. Help them rejoice and see my favor, comfort, and release. Travel worn and burdened down, their hearts shall respond to the awesome sound of freedom and love released to their hearts. They shall know and rejoice at their brand new start. And as they revel, My Spirit receive, they shall forget the times that they grieved. They shall go forth with hearts filled with love, with song and with praise, straight from above."

MIGHTY PLANS!

Does the Lord REALLY have mighty plans for each one of us? Is that word for everyone or just those famous people?

If that's what is going through your mind right now, take this into consideration: David was just a shepherd. Probably a very smelly one. He was skinny, his skin was ruddy, and he did not look much like a powerful man. Yet because of his faith, he killed predators that attacked his flock, and a giant predator who had killed his countrymen. And he did it without fancy armor or chariots.

Moses stuttered and was self-conscious about it. So God gave him Aaron as backup. Barak wouldn't go to battle without the Prophetess/Judge Deborah because she had favor with God. Mary, by faith, endured the shame of being pregnant before wedlock. Abraham lied. David committed murder. Moses, too, committed murder. Samson fell into sin. Paul killed Christians in the name of God. The woman of Samaria was living in sin with a man not her husband. Peter, James, and John were fishermen—a low class job in that day. They also were a little "thick" about getting Jesus' teachings and warnings. Yet God had something special for each of them because of their faith—because of their love for God. And in spite of their weaknesses.

All of us are weak in an area of our lives. In our weakness, HE is our strength. All we have to do is love Him first, and love our neighbors next. Not always simple, but always necessary. He will take our hearts and use us for His Kingdom and all we have to do is say, "Yes!"

Love, Faye

Day Twenty-four

"As the Father loved Me, I also have loved you; abide in My love.
If you keep My commandments, you will abide in My love,
just as I have kept My Father's commandments and
abide in His love. These things I have spoken to you,
that My joy may remain in you, and that your joy may be full."

JOHN 15:9-11 NKJV

EXCERPT FROM *WALKING ON WITH JESUS*:

"The world looks for standardized Christianity (rules and regulations). I have come to set all free. Two rules I have given. Love the Lord your God with all your mind, body, soul, and spirit; and show that love to your brothers and sisters. Stalemates are broken and lives set free in the presence of that kind of love. Seek the Giver and not the gifts, and the gifts will be yours to bestow upon my people with love."

GOD'S VERY BEST

A dear friend once shared with me about a struggle she had been experiencing with eczema. Eczema is a nasty skin problem that not only is contagious, but painful, and seems to hang on for a long time. She is a mighty prayer warrior and mature Christian in the faith. It seemed as though the problem would not leave. THEN she went to church one Sunday and a little boy grabbed her hand and asked if he could pray for her. He did, and within a few days the eczema had cleared up!

Sometimes children catch the fire quickly. Why did God answer the little boy and not my friend? Actually, He did answer her prayer too! The beauty of God is that He answers our prayers in His way, just not according to our timetable or method. And He makes it so that everyone's prayer is answered, even when two are asking for the things separately.

Once in my office, we hired a wonderful Christian sister. I had prayed and prayed that we would hire her, as she was a joy to work with. She would lay hands on her typewriter (before computers) and pray that it would work. She would hug people and bless them, and leave every-one smiling. And God answered my prayer. Less than a week AFTER we hired her, she quit, and was hired by another city. The new job had better pay for her family and better benefits for her son. God answered my prayer, but then He answered hers too. Even though I was disap-pointed, she obtained what she needed from the Lord. A year later, she had a massive traffic accident. Without the benefits she had obtained at the new job, she would have been left destitute with no help for her son. God knew the end from the beginning.

The gifts of God are for the people. They aren't ours, they are God's, given to show forth His love. If we finally get a grip on that, He will release His power through us as His vessels and mighty things will happen! It's not about us, it's about Him. It's about His purposes and plans, revealed through His people. He always knows the best way to answer when we call...and answer He ALWAYS will!

Know that God has already answered your heart cries. If you are going through some difficulties, know that the Lord's very best answer is coming for you. He loves you!

Love, Faye

Day Twenty Five

"The LORD is at the head of the column. He leads them with a shout.
This is His mighty army, and they follow His orders."

JOEL 2:11 NLT

EXCERPT FROM *THE SINGING BRIDE*:

*"Stretched across the sky, a banner, calling forth the Army of the Lord. Calling
out the strong and stalwart, warriors that have conquered by the Word. Have
you heard the call and answered, marching with the Army of the Lord? Side by
side we're marching together, bringing forth the victory of His Word. We have
learned to march forth together, bringing forth the victory of His love. Now we
shall be one together, conquering the foe on every side. Standing by our faithful sisters and brothers, side by side, the Lord's most holy Bride."*

A UNIFIED ARMY

Have you ever wondered how an army could walk together and be
in unity when they don't really know each other? Ouch! The vast majority of Christianity goes to church on Sunday, maybe to some conferences, maybe a dinner or two, but we don't really know one another. We
know ABOUT each other, much like people know ABOUT Jesus, but
don't know Him intimately. We're busy you know. And our pastors are
speakers so they are busy, too. Spending time with each other is more
important than we will ever realize. Being loving and vulnerable, making
an effort, staying humble with each other is a healing fountain of life.

I have a dear friend who was single for many years and went to a
large church. She was sort of an "outcast" because she was single with
children. For some reason, few members of the church would spend time
with her. This also may have been because she was not of the same race
as they were. But she felt lonely and isolated from the people in the pew.
She and I spent lots of time together, and her faith helped me through
some lonely times of my own. When I wanted to tell the Christian
church to drop dead, she actually dragged me kicking and screaming to

that same church… and it turned out to be a giant blessing and a place of healing for me. She kept her heart from bitterness against the very people who had left her feeling alone… and it saved me from a big root of bitterness too. But the fact remains that they should have made an effort at friendship.

One day, a special friend came over to the house and we made cookies and candy together. God bless her—she helped me so much and out of it she received a few plates of gifts to give away. She told me that no one had ever invited her to do that before. Help us, Lord! I'm so thankful she is my heart friend!

The Body of Christ was created by the Lord as a place of heart friends. It is to be ONE as the Father, Son, and Holy Spirit are one (John 17). We can't live as one if we don't form loving relationships, meant to last through eternity. If we are looking for perfect people to love, the only one perfect is Jesus. If we find fault with everyone and push them away because we are too busy or don't really want to get too close, we miss the point. If we don't have relationships, we can't be His Army. If we don't love, we can't be His Army. We're not an "army of one." We are the Army of The One who died for us. And if we love one another as He loves us, we really will conquer all that comes our way, and it will keep us from the heart conditions that kill us.

May you have many heart friends—people you can trust, people you can pray with and for, people who will stand at your side and fight for you when the going gets rough. And may you find the love of Jesus in relationship to Him AND the oneness of the true Bride of Christ!

Love, Faye

Day Twenty-six

"Your love delights me, my treasure, my bride. Your love is better
than wine, your perfume more fragrant than spices."
SONG OF SONGS 4:10 NLT

EXCERPT FROM *WALKING ON WITH JESUS*:

*"Forgiveness is the key to cause the enemy to flee. Stolen ground is his to grab.
He'll always take a stab. Release his hold by being bold to stand in forgiveness
and say, 'I refuse to be offended this day.'"*

THE FRAGRANCE OF LOVE

Fragrance is one of those words we don't think much about when we
go about our daily lives. But Christianity often gives off something other
than a "fragrance of Christ." We are offended easily—by our govern-
ment, by our brothers and sisters, by our co-workers. Most people know
what we don't like and what we are against, but rarely experience the
love of Jesus through us.

Today's excerpt from Rosalie's book may seem short, but it is
extremely profound. Forgiveness is the fragrance of Christ—it is His
main purpose: to forgive all that stands between mankind and God, so
that we can be together with Him for eternity.

In the 80's, two of my closest friends and I had a split. The situation
between us became volatile because we were both angry. We were both
offended that the other didn't understand why we did what we did. We
were giving off the stench of unforgiveness.

Like a ball and chain wrapped around my ankles, my anger and hurt
kept me from joy for several years. I easily cried, obsessed with anger,
and felt like a tree stump dead in the forest after a forest fire. I had no
hope or life in me. I hated Christians for the hypocrites I thought they
were. Until one day, as I prayed and sought my Father for forgiveness
for them and for myself, all of the pain and sorrow fell away. Like being
washed with clean fresh water, it disappeared and never returned. Today

my friendship with those people has been fully restored, and all the offense and hurt is gone!

Let us take a check of our hearts to see if what we give off is fragrance or unforgiveness. It can mask itself as judgment, offense, or opinion. It can sound like whining. It can come out as gossip. The fragrance of Christ is love and forgiveness, clean and pure. It is the love that takes no thought of what people say or do, but only what can be given to help them be refreshed and lifted into the Presence of Jesus. If someone is hurting or in sin, we can woo them with the fragrance of Jesus' love or push them away with the stench of judgment. May all of us be that smell of fresh-baked bread, the bread of forgiveness!

Love, Faye

Day Twenty-seven

"Whatever you ask in My name, that will I do, that the Father may be glorified in the Son. If you ask anything in My name, I will do it."

JOHN 14:13-14 NKJV

EXCERPT FROM *A WALK WITH JESUS*:

"Remain in my love. Remain in the brightness, splendor, and immenseness of my love, for it encompasses all creation. It enlarges and grows and totally engrosses those who allow it to grow within them. Once it takes root, it grows, and nothing can stop it. There is no fear within that love. When there is fear, that light has not been allowed to shine, purify, protect, and rise above all obstacles. Remain in that love, and all else falls into place."

OVERWHELMED?

How do you pray for things or people's circumstances that seem impossible?

For people, we do it by loving them, one person at a time, one soft prayer at a time. For things, we do it by placing our hands on the computer screen and just asking the Lord to take care of it. Simple? Yes! But in the case of people, it can sometimes look anything but simple!

Throughout the Bible we have many examples of folks who were occasional idiots. Moses lost his temper and killed a man. David let his testosterone run away with him and killed a man to get his wife. Abraham and Isaac lied to cover themselves and almost got their wives in a dangerous situation. Samson made a hash of his life by being attracted to an evil woman. Solomon, the "wisest" man in all of history, had 600 wives, who caused him to allow false idols throughout his territory. What a mess! How could those men ever have been favored by God… and yet they were!

God loves a challenge. He loves people so much that those who adamantly proclaim things that sound mean and nasty are in for a real surprise…God hears our prayers for them! They are toast for the Kingdom of Heaven!

I once had a boss who many people disliked. He was crass, hot tempered, and could be vicious. Some on the city council detested him within the first few months of his hiring. Some of the men on the police force thought he was the southbound end of a northbound donkey. But I noticed something in spite of all his bluster. When he talked about people—the citizens who had been hurt, or his own men, tears would form in his eyes. He'd gruffly blink them back and walk away so no one would see. But the tears were real. By the time he left from the position some months later, he was joining us on occasion for prayer. He honored me—and thereby honored the Lord in me. I consider him a friend to this day. He was never hopeless, nor was he as gruff as he seemed—God had a pry bar in his heart. There is softness towards the Lord underneath the grizzly bear exterior.

When you encounter overwhelming prayer requests, don't be dismayed. God knows the needs, all He asks is that we ask for them. It doesn't take more than a minute, and our prayer doesn't need to be long or drawn out. He is the ONLY true and living God. He hears every prayer and He answers them. It's like setting in motion an unstoppable avalanche when we pray. All of the junk is going to get shoved down the hill and the only thing left standing is what God wants. It's a true adventure in changing lives!

Love, Faye

Day Twenty-eight

"So don't worry about tomorrow, for tomorrow will bring
its own worries. Today's trouble is enough for today."

MATTHEW 6:34 NLT

EXCERPT FROM *WALKING ON WITH JESUS*:

"Hang on to your dreams. Go forth with the promises ringing in your heart. Press forward to attain the prize. Leave behind all that encumbers and be buoyed up by My Spirit. Be one with My Spirit through trust and reliance. Move in trust. Have your very being steeped in trust of Me, loosed that I might do my will through you. Blessings abundant are yours."

HANG ON TO THE DREAM!

Hang on to your dreams. Yet don't fixate on tomorrow. Dad's ways are often confusing to us as we navigate life on a daily basis. So what is He talking about?

Let's start with a hint: prophecy is not fortune-telling. Prophetic utterance is speaking forth the Word of the Lord—for encouraging the Church, for letting people know that God hears them, for establishing God's will and plan. Sometimes "prophecy" ends up as divination—*will I be married, will I get rich, will such and such be in my future?* It becomes a forum for trying to make God tell us what we want to hear.

Hanging on to our dreams is about hearing the voice of God and staying true to Him, no matter what happens to try to deter us from His plan. A prophetic Word from the Lord can help us stand strong in the midst of the enemy's attempts to derail our destiny.

Every year promises to be more difficult in the world. But God's people are beloved—and His promises to them are yes and amen! We don't need to worry about what is to come or what will happen to us, because our God has promised to be our Rock, our fortress, our strength, our joy... and we are citizens of His Kingdom, not the earth!

God's Kingdom cannot be stopped. Every evil can try to stamp out Christianity or destroy our destinies, but God is sovereign over all. The authority against ALL the works of the enemy belongs to Jesus the Christ. Trust Him. Know that He is King of kings and Lord of lords. And no matter what we see each day, trust Him that His plan and purposes will come to pass in our lives.

Love, Faye

Day Twenty-nine

"We use God's mighty weapons, not worldly weapons,
to knock down the strongholds of human reasoning
and to destroy false arguments. We destroy every
proud obstacle that keeps people from knowing God."

2 CORINTHIANS 10:4-5 NLT

EXCERPT FROM *A WALK WITH JESUS*:

"Once again the forest was cleared of the slag, and you are free to lift your branches high and soak in the sunshine of my smile. Maintain a constant vigilance. Keep the slag cleared out. Any time your focus keeps being drawn away from Me against your will, know that slag is cropping up and needs to be immediately dealt with and cleared away."

CLEANING UP THE MESS

In the excerpt for today, the Lord admonishes us to keep the "slag" cleared out. Slag is the trees that have died or been broken off during harvesting and fallen to the forest floor. While over time they will become soil, if too many of them pile beneath the healthy trees, they become a severe fire hazard. Foresters generally pile the slag separately and burn them to keep the forest clear.

It works the same way in our spiritual lives. Distractions, looking at the wrong things, can keep our focus miles away from where it belongs. Then we miss the excitement and joy of receiving the Father's blessings.

A dear friend shared with me an experience her husband had one day that further illustrates this point. He was hiking through the woods and looked down a canyon. He saw something flying that was partially black and partially white. Since he was walking somewhere near our local dump, he thought, *Oh! That must be a crow flying with a white garbage bag.* He looked closer and realized it was a bald eagle! The revelation came to him—*I've been looking at the garbage of life so much, I missed the majestic blessings!*

God has many blessings for us—but it's up to us to keep the brain clear of stuff that gets in the way. Focusing on the problems always blinds us to the solutions. Allowing the "slag" to pile up places us in danger of more problems. May you have a clear pathway, free of slag, free of distractions and things which block us from the blessings of God!

Love, Faye

Day Thirty

"'For My thoughts are not your thoughts, nor are your ways
My ways,' says the LORD. 'For as the heavens are higher than
the earth, so are My ways higher than your ways, and My thoughts
higher than your thoughts. For as the rain comes down, and the snow
from heaven, and do not return there, but water the earth, and make
it bring forth and bud, that it may give seed to the sower and bread
to the eater, so shall My word be that goes forth from My mouth;
it shall not return to Me void, but it shall accomplish what I please,
and it shall prosper in the thing for which I sent it."

ISAIAH 55:8-11 NKJV

EXCERPT FROM *A WALK WITH JESUS*:

"Let not your heart be troubled. Let not your mind devise plans that I am not in. Let Me form each day from nothing. Let Me be the Master Mind. Choose whom you will serve and follow. Choose my perfect plan as it unfolds or choose deviations devised by you. It is so simple when left to Me and so complicated when the human mind takes over. Open your heart to your Savior, and let Me bring forth unto perfection each moment, each day. You shall see. You shall see and be pleased."

CALM IN THE MIDST OF TURMOIL

"Let not your heart be troubled."

Not easy to do when circumstances are stacked against us. But God has a plan and a way of doing things that tends to run counter to how we see it or how we would do it.

Example: One recent year, north Idaho received a record snowfall. We had several feet within a 24-hour period. The reindeer decoration in our front yard was so buried that only the tips of Rudolph's antlers showed above the snow bank. It seemed awful to some. But the subsequent summer produced bumper crops of food. The fruit trees produced way over their usual amount of fruit. The huckleberry bushes in the forests of

Idaho were thick with luscious, large berries. Our tomato plants went wild with fruit. The snow cover from the seemingly harsh winter brought enough much needed moisture to yield a wonderful harvest.

I have contact with many Christians of every different ministry focus. Many who are warriors are frustrated with the way the world and the nation seem to be going. They run the spectrum from angry to discouraged because it seems as though their prayers are not being answered. But I have good news: let not your heart be troubled. God is still on the Throne. What we think we see is not what God worries about, nor what He has planned for the end game!

God works through His purposes, His way. Remember that He sees the end from the beginning. He commands us to stand for righteousness, to pray as He directs, to be who we are called to be and not compromise. But how He answers our prayers is not up to us. His purpose always involves the souls of the people, and it always involves His Word. When we become upset over what we see, we are not sitting in heavenly places nor praying there.

How did the Apostles keep their faith when Jesus was arrested, crucified, then left them when He ascended? They were afraid. They didn't really understand the circumstances, though the Lord told them to wait for the power to come. They huddled together, praying in the Upper Room (the top floor of a house). They didn't know what was going to happen. Then *pow*! The Holy Spirit blew through their lives and changed everything.

They didn't all suddenly get rich or get a TV show. They didn't all suddenly become well-liked and have fawning followers. They did, however, suddenly become well-known—and within one day's time, 3000 souls were added to the Kingdom of God. Suddenly they could do the miracles Jesus did and many were healed. Suddenly they became targets of the Romans and the Jews. Life got dangerous and complicated in human terms, but powerful and exciting in spiritual realms! What they did, what they experienced, and what God told them to write has had eternal consequences!

We are the adopted sons and daughters of the one True Living God. Our lives have eternal consequences! We are privileged to be called to rule and reign with Him. But that job description gets complicated if we let our minds do the thinking. Don't let the things you see discourage your heart—remember that God Almighty has called you as His own and that He is sovereign over whatever happens on the earth. He will accomplish His purposes in spite of the ravings of the enemy or the foolishness of men. All you have to do is trust Him, keep your mind firmly on His heart, and your faith helmet solidly in place. His grace and love will make up the difference! You are greatly beloved!

Love, Faye

Day Thirty-one

"Love (God's love in us) does not insist on its own rights
or its own way, for it is not self-seeking; it is not touchy or
fretful or resentful; it takes no account of the evil done to it
[it pays no attention to a suffered wrong]."

1 Corinthians 13:5 amp

Excerpt from *Walking On with Jesus*:

"Trust not in humans. Put your trust in Me! Do not expect what they cannot give. Repent and go on. The wages of sin (bitterness) is death. Repentance brings life. Repent and rejoice in Me. Lighten your load as you go along. Carry not that which was not meant to be carried. Take it not to yourself. Repent for the immediate hurt and give it to Me. Then go your way rejoicing. It is no fun to poke at someone who refuses to be hurt. When you turn on them with like responses, they are justified. That is why I say, love and turn the other cheek. Anger cannot feed on such an environment. It can feed upon itself, but not upon you. Keep your spirit pure before Me. Do not give anger or bitterness a moment to breed."

Dependence on God

Whether we are married or single, one of the most difficult attacks comes with bitterness towards someone else. Married couples experience this frequently—and if not handled it will eventually spell disaster, just like it does in the church.

Today's excerpt hits the nail on the head: when we expect something from another human, we are going to be disappointed. When our dependence is on people instead of God, we become angry when they don't do what we want. It is about what WE want. When we trust the Lord, we can rest and be at peace, because He is then in control.

When my husband and I were married, we didn't have enough money to buy a wedding ring, so I made one out of old gold and an old diamond from my mother's ring. Because the gold was very old and brittle, it broke within the first year. Now, of course it was disappointing. But it wasn't a place where bitterness should grow! And so I placed my trust in the Lord to provide a ring someday at His convenience. If I had focused on my loss, it would have placed an unfair strain in our home. One of my favorite statements came from a former pastor: "Ask yourself—is it a big enough hill to die on?" My lack of a ring was definitely not big enough. For me to have thought so would have brought condemnation and embarrassment to our home!

We should not be easily offended or hurt (1 Corinthians 13). We should be able to tell the difference between something worthy of discussion and something that will tear apart a relationship. Bitterness always tears things apart and speaks of our control and selfish desire more than our concern for the hearts of others. It's about God, not about us. It's about love. Let's celebrate love, let's walk forward without the baggage of bitterness!

Love, Faye

Day Thirty-two

"You shall love the Lord your God with all your heart, and with all your soul, and with all your mind (intellect). This is the great (most important, principal) and first commandment. And a second is like it: You shall love your neighbor as [you do] yourself."

MATTHEW 22:37-39 AMP

EXCERPT FROM *WALKING ON WITH JESUS*:

"The world looks for standardized Christianity (rules and regulations). I have come to set all free. Two rules I have given. Love the Lord your God with all your mind, body, soul, and spirit; and show that love to your brothers and sisters. Stalemates are broken and lives set free in the presence of that kind of love. Seek the Giver and not the gifts, and the gifts will be yours to bestow upon my people with love."

THANK GOD FOR STICKY SITUATIONS

I don't know if you've noticed, but loving one another is about as easy as peeling a sea urchin. There are a lot of sharp things that can stab us. Loving God is easy—He IS love, so His response is always gentle, kind, and fulfilling. Loving people often requires leather gloves to keep from getting hurt.

One day when my husband and I drove into the driveway, we noted that our "condo" birdhouse was full. The birds had taken up residence and were fully engaged in nest building. The funny thing is, every "apartment" was taken by a different kind of bird. The top one housed a chickadee, the middle floor a sparrow, and the basement held a pine siskin. They sat happily on their perches, singing sweet bird songs, enjoying the safety of the nest that kept them high above any predators. They didn't seem to care that they were different "denominations." They were just thankful for a place to live that was protected and safe!

Part of the secret to getting along with people is being thankful. I am thankful more than words can express for the friends in my life. It is their prayers and encouragement that keep me going. We can co-exist in peace because we know that we love each other, even through difficult times. We don't have to be jealous, envious, or demand things of each other, because we are thankful for who we are and that we have Jesus. Like the birds in my front yard, it doesn't matter about our differences.

One of these days, Jesus is going to return for His Bride. He's going to see if we have been selfish "bridezillas," or if we have learned how to find the unity of the Holy Spirit. We will never truly agree on doctrines, practice, etc. But we should be able to love with thankful hearts and sense the Presence of God in each other. Today let's allow thankfulness to spread through us. Let's enjoy the goodness of God in each other and let go of all the things that we think we know. We can travel the road to destiny together, and sing our heavenly songs of love with joy!

Love, Faye

Day Thirty-three

"O God, listen to my cry! Hear my prayer! From the ends of the earth,
I cry to you for help when my heart is overwhelmed.
Lead me to the towering rock of safety, for you are my safe refuge,
a fortress where my enemies cannot reach me. Let me live forever
in your sanctuary, safe beneath the shelter of your wings."

PSALM 61:1-4 NLT

EXCERPT FROM *A WALK WITH JESUS*:

"My child, gather your strength around you, and don't let go. Let My Word to you be your strength and your shield and the battering ram against which nothing can penetrate. Surround yourself with my truth and my song to you. Sing and shout, for the day breaks forth, and you shall stand forth straight and tall and alert in My Spirit, in my army of believers who are the standard bearers. Lighten your way through the peace of My Word to you. Bring forth abundant peace to those you touch, through the truth of My Word to you. Sing, for the night passes and the new day dawns, bright, clear, and radiant, through the peace, truth, and strength of My Word to you. Race not into the new day, but take each new day as it dawns, letting each new day work its weight of gold in you."

HOPE FOR TOMORROW

While the whole Bible is filled with honesty, the entire book of Psalms is probably the most honest of them all. All of us can relate to David, who goes through sorrow, anger, and joy as he traverses different parts of his life. In all of it, he comes back to trust the Lord and reminds himself that God is the One who takes care of His people.

One of the most difficult things to do is stand in joy, praise, song, and hope when everything around us is falling apart. Often our joy is stolen by the circumstances. My second year in Christ, I was in such a bad situation that my countenance was continually sad. I was broken and felt like what I can only term as a wilted flower. It was as if I had been cut down and had no source of strength, even though I loved the Lord. In time, God walked me through the "valley" and I grew closer to Him. But it was not an easy time, and it was not a time for Christians to decide I was worthy only of condemnation. Yet some did. Thank the Lord for those who chose to encourage instead of condemn.

Many of our brothers and sisters are in that place right now. We only need listen to the prayer requests around us to know that circumstances in the earth are meant to destroy us. How do we stand? We stand by praise. We stand by faith. We stand by the love of our fellow Christians. When we are going through troubles, it is not the time to judge one another. It is not the time to manipulate, condemn, or demand from one another. It is the time to pray, love, encourage and help back onto their feet those who have been attacked.

When the heart is in sorrow, keep in mind nothing works normally. I laughingly say that my brain cells are on vacation and they have left no one in charge. When the mind is occupied with trouble, it needs all the help it can get to function correctly. We are that help. We are the Army of the Living God. We are the bearers of His love to one another. We are the bearers of His peace to the broken. There is hope for all who love Him!

Love, Faye

Day Thirty-four

"But I have trusted in Your mercy; my heart shall rejoice
in Your salvation. I will sing to the LORD,
because He has dealt bountifully with me."

PSALM 13:5-6 NKJV

EXCERPT FROM *WALKING ON WITH JESUS*:

"Speak to Me your worries and concerns. Stand tall, erect, and confident of my respect and love for you. Showers of blessings shall be revealed to you and you shall understand your calling from Me. Stand still until I release you to move. Consecration is first.

"Trials lie ahead, but they shall be fashioned by my hand, so fear not but rejoice in the God of your salvation. Let this faith be in you that overcomes the world. Safe and secure you shall be as you seek my face and speak forth my words to set the captives free. Surefooted strength is my gift to you brought forth from the furnace of affliction."

"He has dealt bountifully with me" (Psalm 13:6 NKJV).

RESCUED!

Just what is "salvation" anyway? It has become a religious word instead of a God-heart word, so let's bring it back to His heart.

The word "salvation" in the Old Testament comes from the word *Y'shuwah*, or *Yeshua*. Sound familiar yet? It means to help, to deliver, to save, to bring victory, to care for the welfare of someone. Its connotation to the recipient is one who is brought to good health and prosperity, free of problems. The source of salvation is outside of the situation, not inside of it. A "savior" can rescue us from sickness, our enemies, or any other catastrophe. In total, the word denotes a full and complete deliverance from everything we face in life on this earth!

The Bible says that Jesus "saved" us by the cross. That simply means He created the avenue where the enemy of our souls can no longer have authority over us. Not only do we have intimate relationship to the God of all Creation, but like a safe zone wherever we go, there is no plan against us that can prosper. Jesus also took back the keys of death, hell, and the grave by His death and resurrection. That means if we encounter a life-threatening situation here on earth, we don't have to worry, because He's already made a place for us with Him forever. We cannot be separated from His love (Romans 8).

When I was a little girl, my dad saw a car burst into flames. He slammed on his brakes, bolted to the vehicle, yanked the female driver out onto the ground, wrapped her in a coat, and flagged down a passing motorist to call the police. When he got home, he smelled like smoke, his coat was charred, and though he told us what happened, it didn't seem to be a big deal to him. Just something that "had to be done."

Jesus' Name means deliverance, rescue, salvation. He IS those things and does them because it is His nature. He doesn't stop and think first, He simply saves. It is the heart of God that none should perish in ANY way. Salvation is something that "has to be done." In His heart, He is love. In His work, He is love. We are saved by His love. Whatever you are facing today—a trial, a joyous moment, a change in direction—know that the God of salvation is on the move in your behalf!

Love, Faye

Day Thirty-five

"Seek Him Who made the [cluster of stars called] Pleiades and
[the constellation] Orion, Who turns the shadow of death or
deep darkness into the morning and darkens the day into night,
Who calls for the waters of the sea and pours them out upon
the face of the earth—the Lord is His name."

AMOS 5:8 AMP

EXCERPT FROM *WALKING ON WITH JESUS*:

> *"The sands of time shall fall one upon the other and cause you to see the whole
> picture unmarred by shadows and assumptions. I have cleared the path for you
> to walk ahead unhindered by bottlenecks or past traumas. Go forth each day
> rejoicing in that day on its own merits. Rejoice in the appropriation of my love
> and go forth rejoicing in the completeness of each day."*

SHADOWS

The Bible has a lot to say about shadows. There are the good kinds
of shadows, like the shadow of refuge from the heat of the desert, or the
shadow of God which is our protection. That word is the Hebrew word
for defense—*tsel*. But there is also the shadow of death. That word is
tsalmaveth. The most familiar passage, Psalm 23, is where we walk
through the valley of the shadow of death and yet we fear no evil. That
shadow actually blocks truth and light; it is our relationship to God that
helps us keep on walking.

Here is what we all need to remember: a shadow is an image that is
cast upon a surface by something that blocks the light. Think about that
for a minute: a shadow blocks God's light, making everything dark
around us. But it is not real.

Remember when the Bible talked about Jesus obtaining the keys of
death, hell (sheol), and the grave? Death cannot come to us—if we have
received Jesus, physical death is meaningless. It is simply a shadow that
hangs over our head and tries to block the pathway before us.

How do we get out from under a shadow in the natural? We either turn on the light or move our position. Darkness is always trying to discourage and distract us. But we can walk through the valleys of our lives knowing that all the negative things we hear are just echoes, shadows of past things that have no meaning now that we belong to the Lord.

In today's excerpt, shadows and assumptions are listed as things which mar the whole picture of God's glory over our lives. So we must turn on the light and come up higher to move our position so that our focus is not on the shadows or things our mind comes up with! In the Scripture for today we can take heart that when we seek the Lord God, He turns those dark shadows into the light of the morning. In other words, He gives us a fresh start every day. Our God is good all the time. His plan for us all is wonderful, joyous, and glorious. So when the shadows try to snuff out the hope, let's join forces to shed light on the subject!

Love, Faye

Day Thirty-six

"So do not worry or be anxious about tomorrow,
for tomorrow will have worries and anxieties of its own.
Sufficient for each day is its own trouble."

MATTHEW 6:34 AMP

EXCERPT FROM *WALKING ON WITH JESUS*:

"Struggle not, my child, to understand the coming events. Let Me filter them through my love and make of them a masterpiece in your life. Struggle not to maintain control over the events in your life. Walk in my peace. I will bring order and understanding and eliminate the unnecessary. You can depend on that. Now go forward with a light heart, depending on my love to bring you through to victory. Let not distractions detain you along the way by bringing depression and disillusionment before you. Resist and destroy their power by My Word of love and the sacrifice of praise. I love you, my child. Let that truth resound in your heart and prevail."

NO WORRIES

There's a television advertisement here in America that shows a dog worrying about his bone. He's so worried that he can't sleep. He tries burying it in the backyard, but still worries. Then he takes it to the bank to a safety deposit box and still can't sleep. He takes it home and gets insurance, then he can stop worrying. It's a picture of what we do!

The most difficult thing in the world is to not worry. Even well known Christians, in their desire to "teach" us what is to come, tend to cause the vast majority to worry. They go over and over again on the negative things until our faith is shaken rather than helped. We watch the evening news and for many, it causes anxiety. Some people have literally stopped watching the news or praying for others because the needs overwhelm them. Here is your word for the day: Let Jesus carry things—don't worry! He is your insurance policy!

Today's excerpt talks about having a light heart in the midst of whatever happens. That can only happen when we pray out of trust and faith instead of fear and worry. Here is the point: does God hear us when we pray? Does He answer? If He hears us, then He answers, because it is who He is—He lives in us! He can't ignore us because He loves us. He lives here—we're His house! Of course He wants us to be a place of peace and safety.

If we truly believe in and have a relationship with Jesus, then we know that He listens even when we can't speak. He knows that our future is good, even when the world is smothered in deep darkness (Isaiah 60). Even when circumstances surround us that seem hopeless, there is no greater Helper than God. All things work together for good for us (Romans 8:28).

If we know that God is listening, if we believe that He hears, then we have no reason to worry. We can move forward with joy because we know the King of kings personally, and He's made the way for us. Even crucifixion, which looked like a disaster, was a triumph for us all. We are destined for victory, no matter what it looks like in the natural.

Love, Faye

"Now this is the confidence that have in Him, that if we ask anything according to His will, He hears us. And if we know that He hears us, whatever we ask, we know that we have the petitions that we have asked of Him." —1 John 5:14-15 NKJV

Day Thirty-seven

"Then the lame shall leap like a deer, and the tongue of the dumb sing.
For waters shall burst forth in the wilderness, and streams
in the desert. The parched ground shall become a pool, and
the thirsty land springs of water;… A highway shall be there,
and a road, and it shall be called the Highway of Holiness.
The unclean shall not pass over it, but it shall be for others."

ISAIAH 35:6-8 NKJV

EXCERPT FROM *A WALK WITH JESUS*:

"Be removed and lifted up. Be removed from the everyday rigors of life, for I have made for you a stream in the desert, a place of refreshing and rejuvenation, to bring forth new life in many others through your coming apart to be with Me and being refreshed. The plans that I have for you shall be revealed step by step, and you shall know of my benevolence and untold blessings toward you. The axle shall revolve with rapidity as you see my plan for you unfold. Sit upon the horse of my choosing, straight and tall in the saddle, proud to do my will, choosing to forsake other paths and willing to follow my way for you. Refreshing is my way for you and resounding with every kind of prosperity and success. Go to it, my child."

PASS THE REFRESHMENTS!

A place of rest, peace, safety, refreshing, rejuvenation. That's what God has for all of us. That's Who Jesus is—His sacrifice gave us the ability to rest our troubles on God so that we can be at peace. In turn, we are to be a place where people can be refreshed.

Unfortunately, the Body of Christ at large is often not a place of rest!

I have many friends who no longer fellowship at a regular church because of rigid traditions, gossip, backbiting, infighting, social-climbing, and too many programs and ministry rivalries. If I were God, I wouldn't want to hang out in those environments either!

We can't change the people around us, but we can change ourselves. Jesus asked us to be salt in the earth. That means we need to flavor the world around us, whether it's the church or the secular people we know. Flavor and preservation are the two "jobs" of salt. Too much salt and the food is inedible, too little and it's bland.

The key to being a place of refreshing is simple: love with the Heart of God and remove your own personal agenda from the equation. Once when I was a drama director, a couple of ladies did everything in their power to get me in trouble. They twisted the facts, outright lied, and tried to cause division in the cast. Then they tried to sway the pastor. Why? Because both of them wanted the position I held, they wanted to be in charge. They had created a place of dissension and upheaval rather than a place of peace and safety. (My wonderful pastor at the time, by the way, when advised of what was going on, immediately took authority and stopped it. It never happened again.)

The world is a harsh place. Our homes and the church need desperately to be a place of peace and safety for everyone. They cannot be places of judgment, strife, fear, or "useless wranglings."

Good managers try to create a safe environment in the workplace, too. Bad managers let it run into stressful areas that harm workers. We, as the Christian members of society, should be the salt that balances the flavor and brings the refreshing of God's love to it all.

Let's forsake the worldly path, and choose the straight one that brings life to others. We are the sons and daughters of the God who gave us refreshing, so let us pass it on!

Love, Faye

Day Thirty-eight

"I tell you the truth, if you had faith even as small as a mustard seed,
you could say to this mountain, 'Move from here to there,'
and it would move. Nothing would be impossible."

MATTHEW 17:20-21 NLT

EXCERPT FROM *WALKING ON WITH JESUS*:

"Be established in Me. Be what I have called you to be. Look up and be confident and rejoice. Be secure in the knowledge of my care for you. Be removed from the problem, for with Me it is no problem. Be resourceful, for I have given you much and called you to much. I will continue to give you the desires of your heart. You shall not want for any good thing. Ascribe unto Me praise and thanksgiving. Together we shall move mountains."

FAITH FROM THE SOURCE

We are called to be mountain movers. We are called to release the River of Life through us. But this is tough to do when there are blocks in our minds and hearts.

My husband and I once visited Lake Foredyce in northern California in the High Sierras. Around the edges of the lake are many small streams. As I walked around our camp one day, I noted that most of the streams stayed connected to the original source and flowed into the lake. But some went off on their own and dried up in the heat. They all started at the gorgeous waterfall upstream, but not all flowed toward the prescribed destination.

Rivers that flow with depth and power are mountain movers. They can go over and around rocks, and even move those rocks out of the way! A deep, rushing, powerful river can change the landscape!

In today's excerpt there is an important statement: "Be established in Me." If we think we are Christians but walk in sin, we are not established in God. If our goals in life are based upon how important we think we are, they are not God's goals. And we are building our house on sinking sand. Our "stream" will not be deep enough to withstand the trials of life and we will dry up because we have not stayed connected to the Source.

The Scripture verse today has an admonition, which was aimed at a demonic deliverance situation. It tells us that it takes the establishment of our hearts in Christ to accomplish great things through His power! False Christians, those who are Christians in name only, will not accomplish His will.

"Mountain movers" in Christ are people who keep themselves closely connected to Him. When they make a mistake and go off the path, they quickly make course corrections and get back to Jesus. They stay clean daily with a heart of love and repentance, thinking about others. They grow deep into the Holy Spirit, keeping His Presence first and foremost in their lives. They are not religious or rigid, nor are they selfish and rebellious. They are free and loving, and they allow that River to go where He wishes. They change the landscape! Let's change the landscape and move those mountains for ourselves and for each other!

Love, Faye

Day Thirty-nine

"For I will look on you favorably and make you fruitful,
multiply you and confirm My covenant with you.
You shall eat the old harvest, and clear out the old because of the new.
I will set My tabernacle among you, and My soul shall not abhor you.
I will walk among you and be your God, and you shall be My people."

LEVITICUS 26:9-12 NKJV

EXCERPT FROM *A WALK WITH JESUS*:

"Ours is a relationship of love, one of mutual respect, for you have known Me in a way that few have grasped. You have seen my hand performing wonders and blessings for you and your loved ones. You have traversed the way with Me, seeking my guidance at every turn and blessing My Name. My child, my love flows out to you strongly. There is no area in your life that my love cannot touch and re-create. Stay close to that love. Draw on that love. Depend on that love. And as you do this, that same love flows from you to others. That drawing and dependence on my love creates a flow of my love from Me to you and to others: a flow that is continuous. Beauty and strength come through my love. All gifts of My Spirit are created through my love. So are your gifts to be, created through my pure love given forth. Stand firm, stand tall in my love, for you are my beloved child in whom I am well pleased."

MAKE WAY FOR THE NEW!

We have an awesome God who turns His face toward us when we love Him and obey Him! The words "look on" in the Leviticus passage from today are translated "respect" in the King James Version, and mean to turn toward, face-to-face. Today's excerpt is about a face-to-face relationship with the Lord. Those who had face-to-face relationships with God in the Bible became the founders of our faith and friends of God.

God does not play favorites. Scripture tells us that "God is no respecter of persons" (Acts 10:34 KJV). God is totally equal in the availability of His love. But He DOES respect—turn to—us when we seek Him and love Him with our whole heart. He honors those who serve Him faithfully in any capacity. Every part of the Body is valued! We can all have a face-to-face relationship with Him and be His friends! (1 Corinthians 12:12-27.)

When I was a child, one of our neighbors had a grain silo that was nearly always full. Once in a while the kids in the neighborhood would climb to the top of the silo and slide down the grain piles to the bottom. We had no concept of any danger, but I did notice one thing: when old grain was in the silo, playing there was just plain nasty. The smell was moldy and rancid. The taste of the air as we breathed it in was unpleasant. I got to the point that, unless they had freshly filled the pile, I wouldn't play there anymore.

Today's Scripture talks about eating the old grain to make way for the new. All of us have "eaten" of the old practices of Christianity that do not make room for those who are called by the Lord. We have all been through the old traditions or teachings which are either just plain wrong or keep us from being God's friend. When mankind tries to be in charge, they tend to hang the veil of the temple back up and try to keep everyone but themselves out. But that veil was torn when Jesus died for us. That open door is for everyone who will receive Him!

It's time for us to clear those old pockets out and let Him fill us with His fresh anointing, with His love which is the "new grain" that brings life. Fresh grain makes great food and accomplishes its purpose: to feed people! The personal, flowing love of God, His Presence, becomes like the new grain that brings life to others.

Love, Faye

Day Forty

"And shall God not avenge His own elect who cry out
day and night to Him, though He bears long with them?
I tell you that He will avenge them speedily.
Nevertheless, when the Son of Man comes,
will He really find faith on the earth?"

LUKE 18:7-8 NKJV

EXCERPT FROM *WALKING ON WITH JESUS*:

"Plant your feet solidly in the security of my love and confidence in my faithfulness. Prizes go to the strong and secure in Me. You have stood strong. Reflect on the many times you have stood through the storm as winds blew with trees toppling all around you, but you stood. Time has stood still in your heart as the world has swirled around you. Time shall take on new dimensions of meaning and fullness. Be encouraged as you see Me move on your behalf and bring into the present the promises of the past that were always for the future. Be encouraged as you stand in that place of fulfillment brought forth by my grace and love. My faithfulness has made it so."

GOD'S GOT IT COVERED!

Jesus often told His disciples that they didn't have much faith. They were always hung up on irrelevant things, like not having enough food, or rough water on the lake, or who was going to sit by Jesus in Heaven. They failed to recognize that the Son of the God of Heaven was in their midst already!

Faith is not about denial of the things we face. We can't "stick our heads in the sand" and pretend there are no problems. Faith knows and believes that God will grant us whatever we need, in spite of what surrounds us. Faith knows that His faithfulness and love outweigh any problem. Faith knows WHO HE IS.

The journey for me in faith has been, like it has for all of us, a rocky up and down one. My name, Dorothy Faye, means "God's gift of faith (trust)." At one point in my life, the only person I trusted was me. I had joined MENSA, a well known group of intellectual "smart" people, and thought I was cool. God got a hold of me while I was a member, and showed me that "smart" meant nothing and His IQ was WAY higher than mine. I noted immediately after meeting the Lord that the people I met in the organization had no faith in anything except their own IQ. I had just come face up with the fact that God was real, and my brains were pretty puny compared to the warm, powerful, life-changing Presence of God!

Over the years, through the trials of life, I have come to the conclusion that the pathway sometimes gets scary, but God hasn't run away from me. The path is scary to me, but not to Him. So "standing while the trees bend around me" is what I try to do. He holds my tears in a bottle of remembrance. He puts His arms around me for a place of safety. He works things out for my good even when it seems that everything is falling apart.

God called each of us from the foundation of the world to be His adopted sons and daughters. We were paid for, redeemed from everything that has tried to destroy that place in history by the Son of the Living God. Cancer cannot keep us from His love. A lack of money cannot stop Him from helping us to fulfill our destiny. His grace is sufficient in all things, and in all things His love abounds. In these things lie the grain of faith needed to please our Lord. Plant it and watch it grow!

Love, Faye

Day Forty-one

"He lays the beams of His upper chambers in the waters, Who makes
the clouds His chariot, Who walks on the wings of the wind,
Who makes His angels spirits, His ministers a flame of fire."

PSALM 104:3-4 NKJV

EXCERPT FROM *WALKING ON WITH JESUS*:

*"Out of sight, out of mind is the way of the world, but not the way of My
Kingdom on earth. My Spirit goes out to heal at any moment of any day, from
my faithful ones who hear the call to love and pray, opening the way for My
Spirit to move. You are a candle lighter. I use you to spark hope, light, joy, and
enlightenment into the lives of others. It only takes a spark to get a fire going.
You are a fire-starter in my people. Bask in My Glory. It gets the fire burning
hotter in your soul, attracting others to partake with exuberance and joy."*

FLAMES OF LOVE

When we talk about our God and fire, we often get the picture of a
mean, angry God coming to earth to kill and destroy His enemies.
Scripture says that our God is a "consuming fire" (Deuteronomy 4:24
KJV). So when God tells us to be "fire-starters" and that He makes His
ministers flames of fire, what does that mean? Do we need to run around
with matches, exacting vengeance for God? Not even close.

When Moses stood before the burning bush in Exodus 3, the bush
was completely engulfed in the flame of God, but it did not burn up.
When he encountered God in that manner, he was changed forever! His
entire outlook, his entire future suddenly became consumed by the God
He had met. In the years after, Moses spent many hours in the tent of
meeting because he was a friend of God.

In metalsmithing, the hottest part of the flame is very near the tip of
the torch. It is there that the flame is hot, and the impurities low. The
closer we are to God when we touch the lives of others, the less of our
own garbage we deposit on them. The more we are consumed by His

love, His fire, the better we will be able to bring them in touch with Him. The picture in all of Scripture is about the closeness of God bringing about transformation.

As servants of the Most High God, we should give out of the pure love of God to be an agent of change to those around us. His powerful gifts, His unconditional love, His Presence, all come as an outgrowth of our love for Him. The miracles, those "burning bushes," those moments that change the lives around us flow from us simply because He is here. Let Him light the flame today!

Love, Faye

Day Forty-two

"For You have been a strength to the poor, a strength to the needy
in his distress, a refuge from the storm, a shade from the heat;
for the blast of the terrible ones is as a storm against the wall.
You will reduce the noise of the aliens,
as heat in a dry place; as heat in the shadow of a cloud,
the song of the terrible ones will be dimished."

ISAIAH 25:4-5 NKJV

EXCERPT FROM *WHEN GOD SPEAKS TO MY HEART*:

"There is peace in the midst of the storm, as you draw on my love to keep you warm. As you rest in my arms, you will know exactly which direction to go. Don't be fearful. You shall not fail. Your life shall not get off track but will continue moving as I have preordained it for you. You will be fulfilled this side of Heaven. You know in your heart of my promises. Trust is not an issue here. Hope deferred has once again caused weariness to set in. But be encouraged! With Me you know you will win! Release the tendency to rely on others to lift up your heart. Instead, look to Me for my peace and confidence. Let Me be the one you call out to, to receive your strength and peace in all you say and do. Drink in My Peace!"

BE A RESCUE BOAT!

Sometimes we have to learn how to get "peace in the midst of the storm." When I was young, my dad built and operated a cruise boat on Lake Coeur d'Alene, Idaho. One night during a cruise, the weather abruptly changed from partly cloudy to torrential rain and thunderstorm. The Coast Guard issued a warning to boaters to get off the lake, so we began the process of turning around to go back to the dock. As we made the wide swing with the big boat, we saw a small recreational boat bobbing in the water. By then, the lightning and thunder was nearly deafening, and was cracking close to us all around that part of the lake. It was beautiful and dangerous all at once.

We came alongside the boat and found a whole family, Mom, Dad, and kids, completely drenched. Their boat had run out of fuel, and their radio was not working. So we "heaved to," tied their boat to ours and rescued them from a stormy night. They were so grateful, they sobbed tears of relief. It made me cry to see them so happy. The storm was stopped in their view, even though the waves and rain and thunder continued on the lake.

I don't know about you, but when storms arise in my life, I'm not always the perfect picture of peace. Sometimes God brings a big boat to rescue us, sometimes we have to swim, and sometimes He stills the waves. But He is always there for us, no matter how He chooses to help us get safely out of the storm.

Sometimes it's comforting to know that others are there with us as we go through the storm! Praying for one another is about doing that: drawing close to people as a help in times of trouble. Sometimes the battles are harder than others, sometimes it's a rejoicing. We are friends, family of God, and we can come alongside each other when things look hopeless. I want to be a rescue boat, how about you?

Love, Faye

Day Forty-three

"Thus says the LORD of hosts: 'Execute true justice,
show mercy and compassion everyone to his brother.'"

ZECHARIAH 7:9 NKJV

EXCERPT FROM *WALKING ON WITH JESUS*:

"Stand forth as an illustration of my faithfulness and an illustration of my inheritance. Favor I have bestowed upon you in the past, and favor shall fall upon you in the present and future. Trust Me to bring forth the right result. Be not ashamed, but stand tall and proud of who I am in you. You are a walking symbol of my grace. You are not alone. Singleness of heart I have given you as a gift. It shall carry you through unscathed. Be at peace and respond with love."

An Illustration of God

What does it mean to be an illustration of God's faithfulness, and even His inheritance? We have been taught religiously that going out to save the world, or speaking at public services, or doing miracles, healings, etc., is what it means to show forth Who God is to the world. While it can encompass those things, it's not the main point.

God is love, and in Him there is no darkness. Scripture says that WE are God's inheritance. The whole purpose of Jesus' sacrifice was so that we can be one with the God who is love! And if we are one with Him, then we should be like Him and allow the Spirit of God to work through us without hindrance. And one of the best ways to show Him to the world is in how we deal with each other.

A true friend is one who loves us in spite of our faults and failings, and who never quits loving us, no matter what happens in our lives. God is like that—He gently draws us back when we make a mistake, and if we don't listen, He still works hard at trying to get our attention. He tirelessly goes after the lost sheep. Are we tireless or do we get cranky and want to give up?

I once had a wolf-mix dog. When we got him from the pound, he was a mess—scared, and terrified of everything. Then he started eating the furniture. I'm not kidding—he ate the couch, several remotes, a pair of earphones, and part of a metal detector. We realized that he must have been abused before being adopted out of the shelter, so we worked hard at making his life better. With some work, he became one of the best dogs we ever owned. The Lord once asked me if I was willing to bring that much love to people. I had to repent, and shortly after my repentance, He told me to start a home fellowship.

Love is patient and kind. It establishes boundaries and imparts strength and hope. It brings friendship and transformation. It builds up people, it does not tear them down. Love changes the atmosphere and lightens the burdens. Love is a place where we literally become the illustration of God's inheritance—the people of God, those who love. Jesus said that His disciples would be known by their love. I pray for you today that His love will drench others as you touch their lives. And may you have many heart friends with whom you can share the wondrous things that God does for you and through you!

Love, Faye

"Then those who feared the LORD spoke to one another, and the LORD listened and heard them; So a book of remembrance was written before Him for those who fear the LORD and who meditate on His name. 'They shall be Mine,' says the LORD of hosts, 'On the day that I make them My jewels. I will spare them as a man spares his own son who serves him.' Then you will again discern between the righteous and the wicked, between one who serves God and one who does not serve Him."
—Malachi 3:16-18 NKJV

Day Forty-four

"Do not remove the ancient landmark
which your fathers have set."
PROVERBS 22:28 NKJV

EXCERPT FROM *WALKING ON WITH JESUS*:

"Landmarks are being approached and passed and much ground traversed quickly. Struggle not with the hardships along the way. They too will be passed quickly. Keep your eyes on the promises and rejoice and be glad, for My Spirit goes with you to encourage and lift you up. Lift up your heart and rejoice this day for the awareness of My Presence shall increase and be as a constant companion of peace and contentment."

LANDMARKS PASSED

In the Book of Joshua, chapter 4, Joshua took 12 stones (one for each tribe) from the the middle of the Jordan River and set them up in the Israelites' lodging place as a landmark, honoring the miracle given by the Lord when He parted the Jordan River for His children to walk through to the other side on dry ground. Landmarks also were used as property boundaries for each clan, and it was considered a sin to move them, just as it is illegal today to move a property marker.

God gives us landmarks in our lives, not to stay in one place, but as remembrances of what He has done in our lives. He never changes! We can use those times, those markers to help us move forward into the new places that God has for us. That's why we shouldn't move these landmarks or throw them out. We must pass them instead.

One landmark day in my own life was a class I had to take for my former job. I've never been a big lover of heights. In planes, I'm fine. Hanging off cliffs or tall objects, not so much. We were required to put on a harness and climb a telephone pole about 38 feet tall. The pole swayed as I started the ascent, which totally freaked me out, even though I was in a perfectly safe harness. I forced myself not to look down, but kept my eyes on the spikes that were the foot and hand rests. As I got to the top, my leg hung up on the last spike and the pole began to sway even more. I couldn't free my leg and fear tried to grab me. Since I could go no further upward, I pushed away the fear and reminded myself that I was in a safe harness. So I jumped! Everyone below me clapped that I had overcome a tremendous fear! I realized that if I could do that, I could overcome anything. It was a landmark day.

All of us are given landmarks in the times and seasons of our lives. We are not to camp by those landmarks, but move forward into the promises of our Lord. God's Presence with us in all that we face will establish His purposes for us. We don't have to fear; we can move forward into destiny!

Love, Faye

Day Forty-five

"It is impossible to please God without faith.
Anyone who wants to come to him must believe that God
exists and that he rewards those who sincerely seek him."

HEBREWS 11:6 NLT

EXCERPT FROM *WHEN GOD SPEAKS TO MY HEART*:

"Let your heart overflow with the goodness of My Spirit. Don't think on past sorrows, but look to the immediate future with joy and anticipation. My heart reigns within your heart. Hearken the rising of a brand new day. Make way for the promise of spring. Await in expectancy for I bring you an uplifted heart, bubbling up with joy and thanksgiving. My abundance is near. Give ear and listen to the coming of My Spirit. Stand strong in the radiance of my smile. I shall lift you up and speak to you My Words of life!"

THE EXPECTANCY OF ABUNDANCE

Over the last several years, we have heard many prophets and speakers talk about abundance from God. We know that in John 10:10, Jesus himself proclaimed that He came to give us an abundant life. So why do we have such a difficult time believing it?

The words "more abundantly" in John 10:10 come from the Greek word *perissos*, which means exceedingly, more than, extraordinary, over and above abundant. Remember the passage that tells us that eye has not seen nor ear heard the wonders God has for us? (1 Corinthians 2:9.) Or the one that promises He will give us more than we can ask or think? (Ephesians 3:20.) He's trying to tell us that if we will just know Him, and trust Him, He will grant us the fullness of His Kingdom, and everything we could possibly need on earth. Our cup will overflow (Psalm 23)!

The problem comes when we attach our ideas onto God's promises. Our idea of abundance often only encompasses being wealthy in the financial sense, or something we may want at the moment of our prayer. God's mind doesn't work like ours, so we get discouraged easily when things we expect seem to fall through. Our expectancy isn't in what God has, it's in what we want.

Your word for today is this: God's Hand of help is here. He is waiting to pour out abundance upon you. Joy, peace, love, redemption, restoration, hope, destiny… all those things He will pour out on you, and more (over and above). His ways may be different than our plan, but His plan will work much better! Get ready to step into the new day prepared for you! It is going to be overflowing with abundance.

Love, Faye

Day Forty-six

"Stand therefore, having girded your waist with truth,
having put on the breastplate of righteousness, and having shod
your feet with the preparation of the gospel of peace;
above all, taking the shield of faith with which you will
be able to quench all the fiery darts of the wicked one."

EPHESIANS 6:14-16 NKJV

EXCERPT FROM *WALKING ON WITH JESUS*:

"Remain under the constant care and abiding love of my outspread wings of protection and direction. Fear not, my little one. Let Me lead and bring forth an abundant harvest in your life with nothing lacking. Silence in your heart the doubts and the fears, for they are not of or from Me. Set your heart and your thoughts on Me and let Me be your perfect guide. What I have started in you I will finish. I will not abandon you. Hold fast your ground. Waver not. I have put within you a singing heart, which shall be revealed in my time."

STAND STILL AND SEE THE SALVATION OF THE LORD

Anyone who has ever operated in the anointing of the Holy Spirit knows that to stand and watch Him do the work is an amazing experience. I was asked to do a short one-person drama one Sunday, and the Lord literally took over. It seemed as though I was watching from backstage! People in the audience started to weep and shout amen, and I had no idea what was really going on. Later, they explained to me what happened—the Lord told the story of the woman with the issue of blood through me... and I was completely clueless. God was my shield and fortress, and He did the performing that touched hearts!

Whatever our appointed task is at the moment, God wants us to let Him do it. Fear always threatens us first—"You can't do it," or "God doesn't want you to do it, you're not worthy," or any number of other negative thoughts are thrown our way like flaming arrows straight to our hearts. In biblical times, flaming arrows were often shot by the enemy. If those arrows came at the shield, they would be ineffective. If there was no shield, death would result. Faith tells us that our God will take care of us, and that knowledge, that understanding, is a shield against everything that threatens us!

Being confident in God's protection and love allows us the freedom to do whatever is necessary for His Kingdom. It allows us the ability to handle any of our personal problems as well. Psalm 91 tells us that if we dwell in God, His wings cover us from anything that may be kindled against us—everything from plagues to terrorist attacks. The operation of His anointing for the gifts of the Spirit works the same way—when we abide in Him, He works through us.

Whether it's an assignment that requires anointing to complete or a situation of spiritual warfare, stand still with your shield and watch God work for you, with you, and through you! Everything He has appointed for you to do will be accomplished.

Love, Faye

Day Forty-seven

"Yours, O LORD is the greatness, the power and the glory,
the victory and the majesty; for all that is in heaven
and in earth is Yours; Yours is the kingdom, O LORD, and
You are exalted as head over all. Both riches and honor
come from You, and You reign over all. In Your hand is
power and might; in Your hand it is to make great
and to give strength to all. Now therefore, our God,
we thank You and praise Your glorious name."

1 CHRONICLES 29:11-13 NKJV

EXCERPT FROM *WALKING ON WITH JESUS*:

*"Perilous times cause frustration and anxiety in the lives of those with no hope.
I have set before you a course of action to bring hope and love to many on the
trail of hopelessness. Continue to strengthen hearts with the freedom of love and
hope. Continue to lift up weary arms with the promise of spring within their
hearts, bringing direction and fulfillment where there was disillusionment and
fear. Release unto Me all weariness and weights. My heart for you has always
been walk with Me and win. And as you pass this simple premise on from heart
to heart, each one will come apart to walk by my side as my faithful Bride. Can
you not see this mighty army marching forth from sea to sea, proclaiming my
love and victory, walking free for all to see? March forth, child of my heart,
unencumbered, flying free, following my lead."*

THE DAY THE EARTH STOOD STILL

The title today isn't referencing an old Science Fiction movie. It's
about victory in the heat of battle. As the Israelites traversed the desert,
they encountered the Amalekites. This vicious army attacked them,
forcing Joshua to lead his people into battle. During the battle, as long
as Moses held up his hands, Israel prevailed. When he put his hands
down, the battle turned against them. So Aaron and Hur sat Moses

down on a rock, and held his hands up so that the battle would be won (Exodus 17).

In the Promised Land, Joshua came up against the Amorites (Joshua 10). In order to finish the battle while daylight allowed them to see, Joshua commanded the sun not to go down, and the moon to stay still for an entire 24 hours. In that time frame, the Lord brought about a victory for Israel. Their enemies literally fled before them, as Israel obviously had the Living God on their side! To us, these were bloody battles, the path to victory, almost weird. Spiritually, however, there is a lesson in them.

In today's excerpt, we find the Lord reminding us that perilous times breed fear and anxiety. They also breed weariness. If the battle is hard enough, we start slipping into darkness and despair, even though we may know the Lord. The solution? Love, unity of spirit, and willingness to lift up the arms of those who are weary, bringing the true power of God that causes light to come into the lives of those who need to finish the battle.

When the Lord asks us to show others the simple truth of His love, it's a call to help others finish with victory. It can be a needed miracle, or a small helping hand, but sometimes the strangest of actions can bring God's power to bear on a problem. Listen for His voice and leadings in these perilous times: the victory belongs to the people of God!

Love, Faye

Day Forty-eight

"For I am about to do something new. See, I have already begun!
Do you not see it? I will make a pathway through the wilderness.
I will create rivers in the dry wasteland. The wild animals in
the fields will thank me, the jackals and owls, too, for giving them
water in the desert. Yes, I will make rivers in the dry wasteland so
my chosen people can be refreshed. I have made Israel for myself,
and they will someday honor me before the whole world."

ISAIAH 43:19-21 NLT

EXCERPT FROM *A WALK WITH JESUS*:

*"My people shall be a praise upon the earth. Bring forth that abundant praise
to Me, that you too may become my praise upon the earth. My praisers are a
mighty force, greater than any force upon the earth, to bring down strongholds
and to open up the way for righteousness to prevail. And prevail it shall! It is
the choice of each individual to be a part of or not be a part of this end-time
army of praisers, my praisers. Open up your heart to Me and let Me fill it with
my radiance and praise. Praise and prevail."*

PRAISE = TRIUMPH, RESTORATION, REDEMPTION

Why does our God want us to praise Him? Is He an ego-maniac?
No, He wants us to praise Him because true praise is an expression of
love. Plus, He inhabits our praises (Psalm 22:3)! The more we praise
Him, the more we pull down the plans of the enemy.

In a practical sense, praising the Lord brings our minds out of our
situation and focuses us on Him. In the spiritual reality, praising the
Lord allows His Presence to flow without interference. It creates a place
of thankfulness in our hearts. And being thankful is also an expression
of love.

Growing up, Dad always gave me whatever I asked for, if it was
within his ability to do so. Is someone hassling you at school? They're
toast. Want a new dress? Go get it. A pretty gemstone? It's yours. Go to

Europe on a trip? Pack your bags. Very rarely did Dad say no, and that was only if what I wanted was dangerous or out of our financial ability. Dad even sold a gun collection to send me to college, and would have done more to send me wherever I wanted to go. Even though as an earthly father he was imperfect and had his moments of malfunction, he loved me and I knew it. For that knowledge alone, I will always honor my dad, even though He is now Home with the Lord. How much more can we honor our Heavenly Father for the love He shows us daily!

Not everyone has such experiences with their earthly father, but the more we know our Heavenly Father, the more we are thankful and filled with praise, the more His Presence will heal all the places we missed from any lack in our earthly parents. The praises we sing give us refuge under His wings. They give us triumph over circumstances. They bring His restoration and redemption to our lives in a River that flows unrestrained through us.

Triumph, restoration, redemption... all are coming soon in a way we never thought would happen. He is doing a new thing and bringing fresh water in the desert just for all of us! Praise His wonderful Name!

Love, Faye

Day Forty-nine

"For the Son of Man will come in the glory of His Father with
His angels, and then He will reward each according to his works."

MATTHEW 16:27 NKJV

EXCERPT FROM *WALKING ON WITH JESUS*:

*"The pages of time are rapidly turning, proclaiming my return. Magnify My
Name, and take not to yourself the Glory of that Name. Reflect My Glory and
call it not your own. Relax and be and I will do in your life. March forth in joy,
but let Me be the teleprompter. Let Me be the inner glow. Let Me be the force
that motivates you to from moment to moment. Let Me be the one to give you
to the world as a gift—and I will in my time. In the meantime, stay faithful to
your calling. Minister my love as never before, for I have called you to love. You
shall shine forth my radiance and draw others to Me."*

THE GIFT

Imagine yourself as Ezekiel in the midst of one of his open visions.
(Ezekiel Chapters 43-47). In these visions, the Glory of God entered
into the temple from the East Gate—the side from which the sun rises.
Then God spoke to Ezekiel about His temple no longer being a place
where kings and religious prostitutes would defile His House, and make
monuments to those evil acts. By Chapter 47, the Lord brought Ezekiel
back to the entrance to the temple, where water was flowing beneath it.
The water that flowed was a life-giving stream, and deep enough that
you couldn't walk through it on foot. It caused trees to grow food every
month and never fail, and their leaves were used for healing. Fish flour-
ished in that vision, which was a sign of God's provision. (Remember the
fish in the New Testament—they provided miracle food, and even coins
to pay the taxes!)

God showed Ezekiel how He planned to give the Holy Spirit as the
River of Life. He also gave him the picture of the believer as the temple.
We are individuals, and governments have no say over our relationship

as the carriers of Christ. Oh, they can try, but they are powerless over relationship to God when that relationship is solid!

Every believer has a purpose that includes being a gift to the Body and to the world, because we are carriers of the Living God! God's Glory is promised as a light to the world (Isaiah 60), and we are the ones who will carry that light. As the temple of the Living God, that River of Life should be flowing from the sanctuary of our hearts all the time. What has tarried for years is now coming to pass. What promises have been delayed are being pushed forward into reality. Let's all be that place of life, healing, fruit, and God's Glory!

Love, Faye

Day Fifty

"Assuredly, I say to you, unless you are converted and become
as little children, you will by no means enter the kingdom of heaven.
Therefore, whoever humbles himself as this little child
is the greatest in the kingdom of heaven."
MATTHEW 18:3-4 NKJV

EXCERPT FROM *WALKING ON WITH JESUS*:

"It's going to be fun, an adventure. See Me place the desire in your heart and be encouraged as you see it come to pass. Stand encouraged. Now is the time to rejoice and go forward in the fullness and radiance of My Spirit. It is truly a new day with new ways. Release unto Me your spirit to soar, for I have given you a spirit of delight, and you shall again delight in all that I bring to you and cause that spirit of delight to be birthed in others. Be refreshed, my little one, and continue on in the journey of life with renewed vision and vigor. I love you!"

ZINNIA ADVENTURES

My Grandmother used to take a lot of pictures of me as a child. One in particular showed me all dressed in red, standing in Mom's zinnia patch, pretending that I was directing traffic. Apparently I wanted to be in law enforcement at an early age!

Growing up in the country was an adventure that I truly miss as an adult. There weren't many people around then, though it's pretty crowded on the river now, so my dog and I would do many "pretend" visits to faraway places… and the garden was a great place to start. My Mom loved zinnias, so she planted lots of them. They were great for my imagination—signs that pointed the way to exotic places like India or Africa. I would imagine a tiger behind the red flowers, maybe an elephant over in the yellow ones. Life was a delightful "zinnia adventure."

As I grew into adulthood, I found a very sad fact of life: adventure is often destroyed by experience, and religious duty replaces the absolute delight of serving the Lord. A lot of the church is heart sick.

Discouragement, disappointment, and hard circumstances have taken a terrible toll on everyone. The entire Body of Christ needs its joy back!

Churches have often traded programs and activities for the sheer joy of ministering to the needy. By the time we've baked our cookies, finished the quilts, prepared or memorized Bible verses and tried to pray, sat through 9 or 10 sermons a month, and spent every night after work at church for two hours, we just want to run away from home! Actual joy got lost in the traffic!

I have some friends who don't know the Lord, but they are joyful and excited about a gentleman in our city who goes to Africa to minister to the children. He is 80 years young, and a US veteran. He sends them photos of his work with the orphanage, and they can't stop talking about it. They are filled with the adventure of his ministry. He's not a big name, doesn't go on TV, and stays within the confines of one little village. He lives with the people and finds delight in what he does and his delight spreads like wildfire through my secular friends. His life is an adventure, and they are captivated by it! He is giving them a "zinnia adventure." He is also planting powerful seeds of the Kingdom in people who need Jesus!

Today's excerpt encourages us to find once again that vision, that wondrous delight in the Lord that speaks of His love for us. Renew today that joy you once had, and step into God's special "zinnia adventures." The desires of your childlike faith will be rewarded!

Love, Faye

Day Fifty-one

"[You are] a fountain of gardens, a well of living waters, and streams
from Lebanon. Awake, O north wind, and come, O south!
Blow upon my garden, that its spices may flow out.
Let my beloved come to his garden and eat its pleasant fruits."
SONG OF SONGS 4:15-16 NKJV

EXCERPT FROM *WALKING ON WITH JESUS*:

"Filtered through my love is everything that comes into your life. Pieces of the puzzle continue to pop up before your face. Patience through the years has been the key. It has brought you to this place of grace. And now into this place which has seen much toil, comes a refreshing fragrance to aerate this soil. Fortunate and to be envied are your comings and your goings. My song of love is upon your lips. Sing it forth with abandon."

GOD'S GARDEN

Sometimes it's tough to see God through circumstances that are difficult. A precious friend asked me once what I used to do for the police department. I'd have to say the best words that describe my years there would be "victory in battle."

God's method of producing fruit is often hard on the flesh (ok, it strips the flesh away). My first few years with the police department were very hard, because in the early 70's, women were just beginning to rise up against tradition, and police departments were not yet ready to accept them as equals. From rear-end pinching to off-color remarks to refusals for specialized training, it took years to gain favor and trust. It happened, but the road was difficult and I had to learn forgiveness, self-control, grace, and patience...and above all, faith. That's not counting the daily exposure I received to the dark side of life—to crime and evil on a large scale. It's like growing a garden with a black bag over the seedlings.

Stereotyping, prejudices, and incorrect ideas ran rampant. Such barriers were hard to break down. Once the barriers were broken by those who fought hard for their place, things became easier. Eventually, our department became one of the first in the state with a female Chief, who happened to be a friend of mine. But this was a hard-fought battle for my friend. She had to "plow" the ground of that garden. She proved herself, and with forgiveness, great patience, and grace, won the place she was destined for all along. She discovered what the above excerpt says, patience and grace were the keys.

The Church at large is no different, but in their case the transition has been slower. Much of this is due to improper understanding of Scripture, but it is a barrier that only God will be able to break down. He does so for each of us: opening doors, changing hearts, blessing and encouraging each of us on a personal level. We must learn patience and faith, and take hold of the grace and love that God wants to grant us. In those things we will triumph over all the problems that ally against us.

The temptation for all of us is to strive, to demand our honor in life's situations. But God has a different way of doing things. It is God who honors us! He asks us to trust Him to open the door. He asks us to love. He asks us to let our gift make a way for us. Striving exhausts, frustrates, and makes us want to quit. When we start trusting the Lord, He rises up to protect us and give us favor!

As God begins to move on your behalf, you will receive breakthrough. You have fought hard and long, and waited for the hope of His calling. You have had thoughts of giving up, but the Lord is near. He is coming to the garden that has been growing in your heart—a garden ripe with patience and faith, forgiveness, grace, mercy, and love. They are His favorite crops!

Love, Faye

Day Fifty-two

"Blessed is the man whose strength is in You, whose heart is
set on pilgrimage. As they pass through the Valley of Baca,
they make it a spring; the rain also covers it with pools.
They go from strength to strength; each appears before God in Zion."

PSALM 84:5-7 NKJV

EXCERPT FROM *WHEN GOD SPEAKS TO MY HEART*:

*"My child, I have formed you and brought you to this place of total surrender
and grace. You have been patient in this place of pruning and grooming, bringing you forth to this new day of provision and new vision. Your cup shall overflow with new blessings. I have prepared you well. My hand of love is here to
guide you, because you are Mine. And now, my precious dove, you shall more
fully reflect my love in everything you say and do, which is my perfect will
for you."*

SURRENDER: FOLLOWING THE HEART OF GOD

There's an old hymn I love to play called "I Surrender All." Once I
goofed and played it during an offering at a large Assembly of God
church. The whole congregation burst into laughter when they realized
what I was playing on the piano. Oops! I didn't mean it THAT way!

The concept of surrender is in Scripture under several terms. Chief
among them is to "turn." Whatever way we are walking, turn to God,
turn around, do it His way. Proverbs 3:5-6 is another surrender scripture, a familiar one: "Trust in the Lord with all your heart; do not depend
on your own understanding. Seek his will in all you do, and he will show
you which path to take" (NLT).

The biblical concept of "surrender" has nothing to do with giving up
in the face of battle. It has to do with the pilgrimage to the heart of God
in our lives. It's turning our face toward His, listening and walking in
His ways, and walking away from our own. In our battles, we are not

told to give up—ever. But we ARE told to just STAND and see God. Stand in trust, stand fully yielded to how God wants to do something.

My life has had some very rocky spots in it over the years. My way of trying to fix those spots has often caused me to run headlong into a wall and not accomplish anything but only make matters worse. Those were broken heart moments where I have watched my own hopes and dreams crumble at my feet. The choice I was faced with was to turn my heart to the Lord for mercy and grace or keep making the same mistake over and over again. These were places of total surrender—to follow His ways, not my own.

I am learning that sometimes to gain everything, you have to lose everything. That place where the heart cannot be consoled by our own will and plans is a place of grace and love from the Lord. In today's Scripture, it's called the "Valley of Baca"—the valley of weeping. When my own plans are hopeless, and tears fill my heart, then God comes in to redeem my life. His Presence, His Holy Spirit, then keeps me stable in the midst of trials that threaten to uproot everything. He has never, ever failed me. He will never, ever fail you. In the place of surrender and grace, His love for you will triumph over anything you see.

Love, Faye

Day Fifty-three

"I waited patiently for the LORD, and He inclined to me, and heard my
cry. He also brought me up out of a horrible pit, out of the
miry clay, and set my feet upon a rock, and established my steps.
He has put a new song in my mouth—praise to our God;
Many will see it and fear, and will trust in the LORD."

PSALM 40:1-3 NKJV

EXCERPT FROM *WALKING ON WITH JESUS*:

> *"Your life is like a song. The melody weaves in and out and comes together,*
> *forming perfect harmony with grace. Each note and word fits perfectly, forming*
> *a beautiful whole. Many never get past the halting, labored opening verse to get*
> *to the fluid chorus. Is it the chorus of a song that gives the most freedom and*
> *joy to the singer and to the listener alike."*

THE SONG OF REDEMPTION

If you have ever been a member of a symphony or band, you know
that there are two things that matter the most—watching the conductor,
and learning the music well. And the only way to learn the music is to
practice.

There was a tiny book written by a Catholic monk named Brother
Andrew called *Practice the Presence of God.* Like music, it requires time
spent with God to get the "feel" of His Presence inside of us. With a
chorus melody, as we play it over and over again, it becomes part of who
we are. Like singing in the shower or humming all day long, hearing the
music of His Presence and His Voice in everything we do…it's how we
become His Song, how His Song of Redemption permeates our lives.

Learning to sing a "new song" is more than just the spiritual singing
of fresh songs inspired by God. It's also a daily freshness of His Presence
in us. As that freshness grows, we become the testimony of Christ. We
become the new song as His glory shines over us and through us. The
shining of His glory is not dependent upon circumstances, it's a showing

forth of His personal love for us in all situations! May your hearts become the Song of Redemption and may the darkness that looms over our lives be pushed aside by the melodies of Christ!

Love, Faye

Day Fifty-four

"They do all their works to be seen of men; for they make wide their phylacteries (small cases enclosing certain Scripture passages, worn during prayer on left arm and forehead) and make long their fringes [worn by all male Israelites, according to the command]. And they take pleasure in and [thus] love the place of honor at feasts and the best seats in the synagogues, and to be greeted with honor in the market places, and to have people call them rabbi. But you are not to be called rabbi (teacher), for you have one Teacher and you are all brothers."

MATTHEW 23:5-7 AMP

EXCERPT FROM *WALKING ON WITH JESUS*:

> *"Strength, love, and compassion come forth unabated when one rests in the comfort of my hand. Rest assured, my child, that the perils, worries, and concerns shall all fall away as you rest in the freedom of my love. Stretched you have been, but the ultimate goal is freedom within my love, not freedom within the love of others. The love and acceptance of others is not the goal. The goal is freedom of understanding and acceptance of the fullness of my love in your life. How others receive and show love is not your problem. You see Me and receive my freshness daily. How they seek, give, and receive is between Me and them. Release, release, release! Shake off the burdens, restraints, and offenses of others. They are not yours to bear."*

THE SEARCH FOR ACCEPTANCE

All of us want to be accepted by others. We don't like to be ostracized or have people hate us. The Pharisees of Jesus' day simply wanted the attention of others—"look at me, the big important person" was their cry. But Jesus told the people that no one is important except God himself, and that all of us are brothers! We are equal in His sight, and if we are equal, then we never need to worry about what others think.

When Job was hit with trial upon trial and even physical problems, his friends judged him. He had no comforter in the process. We all fear that place where everyone stands away from us when we are struggling, so we tend to seek out acceptance from others so that we will not have to face that feeling of being alone. But there is a difference between being accepted and loved by God's people, and seeking to please men. Our love for others is supposed to be unconditional, not based upon how "important" we are!

While in college, one of my instructors told our class that if we continued to take the courses for law enforcement, we would face the hatred of others. Wearing a badge gives a sense of control and power, and conveys a sense of "importance." I was from a small town in north Idaho and had led a fairly sheltered life. My instructor assigned me to a duty that placed me directly in the path of angry college students and citizens. People spat on me. People tore up my warning tickets and threw them in my face. They called me some really choice names. What would my decision be—would I continue on in law enforcement or change directions? I chose to stay the course, and over the years with the Lord's grace, I learned how to turn those experiences into the courage to face down evil. It no longer mattered whether people liked me or not! I had the God of the universe at my side!

There are many wonderful people who do not want to be Christians simply because they are afraid of the consequences among their friends. There are many Christians who seek to please men to get the accolades and receive followers. But God asks us to follow Him simply for the sake of His love!

His love is totally unconditional! His love is gentle and kind, but He also protects and keeps us in the midst of whatever we face. Whether or not people like us doesn't matter, because the God of all creation loves us and wants to hold us close. He covers us under His wings, and comforts us with the sound of His voice. His love changes our entire life—it gives us strength, courage, faith, hope, and joy in the midst of living on the earth. Today may you live in the love of the Lord, bringing life to others and not worrying about the outcome. May He grant you His Presence to comfort you, and the courage to face all that He has laid before you. Above all, may you know the loving acceptance of the Lord God Almighty!

Love, Faye

Day Fifty-five

"When you pass through the waters I will be with you,
and through the rivers they will not overwhelm you.
When you walk through the fire, you will not be burned
or scorched, nor will the flame kindle upon you. For I am the
Lord your God, the Holy One of Israel, your Savior...Because you
are precious in My sight and honored, and because I love you,
I will give men in return for you and peoples in exchange for your life."

ISAIAH 43:2-4 AMP

EXCERPT FROM *WHEN GOD SPEAKS TO MY HEART*:

"Walk in your life—freely. Live a life of abundance. Stand back, survey, and forgive. It is a testament of My Spirit residing and acting in you. Daily cleanse your heart of all the built-up debris. Don't allow the day to pile up, surround, and overpower you. Discard it all. Go forth this day, determined to be my clear channel of love, free from all bondages. Lay down your life before Me. Minister life to those around you! Build up their hearts, and they shall see the glory of their God. Walk in my goodness, live freely, and be unencumbered. You are precious to Me!"

MAKE WAY FOR THE RIVER!

A few years back, our area had a larger-than-normal spring runoff. The snow all melted at once and the rivers overflowed their banks. There is a small dam in our area, and the water flowed so hard and fast that it threatened to overwhelm the gates when all sorts of debris rushed to the edge of the dam and clogged up the river. It would have been extremely dangerous to try and remove the logs that jammed themselves into the gates of the dam.

What we always need to remember is that it's the water flowing through the dam that powers the turbines that make electricity. The river is the source of the power. The River of Life is the POWER SOURCE!

When we have debris in our lives, God's abundance gets jammed up at the gates of our heart. The River of Life is meant to flow freely, powerfully. Water is so powerful that it literally carves out space for itself. It moves rocks, it creates landscapes. But when we leave that river clogged with "logs" it gets pooled and doesn't move in the full power for which it was intended.

The Lord has granted us abundance (John 10:10). Abundance of friends, abundance of Spiritual gifts, and abundance of relationship to the God of the universe! He provides for our needs, even when we'd rather win the lottery. He knows everything about us, everything we could ever desire. And as a loving Father, He makes sure that we are fulfilled. It's just up to us to keep the logs out.

No matter where you are today, the abundance of the River of Life is about to flood your life. Let's all remove any debris that may be standing in the way of God's fantastic power! God is with us and that makes for an abundance we can't contain!

Love, Faye

Day Fifty-six

"Then your light shall break forth like the morning,
your healing shall spring forth speedily. And your righteousness
shall go before you; the glory of the LORD shall be your rear guard.
Then you shall call, and the LORD will answer;
you shall cry, and He will say, 'Here I am.'"

ISAIAH 58:8-9A NKJV

EXCERPT FROM *WALKING ON WITH JESUS*:

"Your light has not been blown out by the storm that blows and rails around you. Fear not that my light will go out, be snuffed out from you, for it will not! It is simply at times on pilot, awaiting the move from my hand to bring it into full flame. But even on pilot, it has that power to warm others and direct them my way. Fear not the seeming coldness of the fire. It is a time of healing and restoration, not a time of giving forth. Be at peace. Be not impatient. Let Me lay the groundwork with strength and correctness. Nothing shall be lost. It is all gain for My Kingdom."

THE PILOT LIGHT

We have a gas fireplace in our living room that serves to heat the entire upper floors of our house during the winter. One night a couple of years ago, a January storm brought 88-mile-an-hour winds to our hilltop. The wind howled through the chimney and ripped off the shingles from the roof, but the pilot light stayed lit! We had to replace the roof, but the house stayed warm. It was amazing.

Evil around us has brought difficult trials to Christians (the "fire" mentioned in today's excerpt), and love in the world grows ever colder (Matthew 24:12). But if we have nurtured our relationship to Jesus and obeyed His Voice, He surrounds us with protection. He keeps our internal "pilot light" lit, even when it seems like everything is collapsing around us. Sometimes, as mentioned in the excerpt above, it is not a time to do anything but refresh and encourage yourself!

Whether we realize it or not, the world is becoming ever more hostile to our faith. We are being blamed for things and lumped together with crazy people. We are being targeted as "hate-mongers" and "dangerous." Evil is called good and good is called evil. It is a time to keep our lamps lit in the midst of darkness and not worry whether the swirling evil will overcome our faith. It cannot do so!

We have the Living God in our hearts and He will keep the pilot light of His Love fully functioning, no matter how rough the storm gets! The storm that tore off our roof could not put out the light. The storms that threaten us cannot remove the Lord from our lives!

Love, Faye

Day Fifty-seven

"Trust in the LORD, and do good; dwell in the land, and feed
on His faithfulness. Delight yourself also in the LORD, and
He shall give you the desires of your heart. Commit your way
to the LORD, trust also in Him, and He shall bring it to pass."

PSALM 37:3-5 NKJV

EXCERPT FROM *A WALK WITH JESUS*:

*"Listen and you shall hear. Retain your sense of expectancy. Delight yourself
in Me, and let that delight shine forth from you. Let your face shine with
Sonshine. The Spark of Life has been rekindled and reigns within."*

HEAR HIS VOICE

There aren't many things more difficult than trying to hear someone
talking to you on your cell phone in the middle of a busy street corner
with buses, cars, and other street sounds blaring around you. The voice
you are trying to hear gets garbled amidst the noise! You end up trying
to get into a building or closing off one ear to silence the cacophony.

In the realm of the Holy Spirit, the secret to getting past the din in
our own heads is to quiet the noise. It takes practice, but it works. One
of the most effective ways of quieting our noise level is to remove the
desperation in our prayer and simply focus on how wonderful our Lord
really is!

He has made the intensity of the sunrise and sunset. Rich with royal
colors, the sky shouts His praise! The stars light the night sky with glorious patterns that pierce the darkness. Babies and animals show forth His
wondrous sense of humor. My dog shows me God's unconditional love.
I smile, my heart quiets, and my ears suddenly open to His still, small
Voice. It's a miracle that never ceases to amaze me!

When we delight in the Lord, we can delight in what He has done
for us, how we met Him, what He has made, what He has promised, or
simply Who He is. This will rekindle that Spark of Life, and the flame

of passion for Jesus will be renewed. Expect His purpose and promise to be fulfilled this year, and move on it. Our God is speaking to all who will listen!

Love, Faye

Day Fifty-eight

"With my whole heart have I sought You, inquiring for and of
You and yearning for You; Oh, let me not wander or step aside
[either in arrogance or willfully] from Your commandments.
Your word have I laid up in my heart, that I might not sin against You.
Blessed are You, O Lord; teach me Your statutes."

PSALM 119:10-12 AMP

EXCERPT FROM *A WALK WITH JESUS*:

*"Attune your heart to My Spirit in the days to come. Speak forth My Words
with spirit and with truth. With boldness, let your way of grace be known, and
proclaim that 'Jesus is Lord, to the Glory of God the Father.' Stand straight and
tall in My Spirit, and let your faith stand solid in Me. We shall go forth with
joy abounding, and good works shall not be found lacking. My Spirit goes with
you, to lead you and guide you. Store up My Word and my peace in your heart,
and go forth with assurance."*

POLISHING THE ARMOR

I hope everyone has noticed that the "heat" has been turned up
against Christians worldwide. Not only overt acts against Christians, but
sneaky underhanded ones too—like financial ruin, severe illness, and
disaster after disaster. Our brethren all around the globe are experiencing difficulties that are deeper than they have been in centuries. Why?
Because we have an enemy who is having a hissy fit. He's mad and he's
looking for ways to attack.

When leaders of nations actively allow sin to run unchecked, those
dark forces have free access—which means that we all need to polish our
armor. This means we need to worship more, encourage each other
more, and exercise our faith more. God's Word—both *Rhema* (God-
breathed to each of us) and *Logos* (Jesus himself and the Bible)—is true
food that connects us to God's Heart, but reading it in written form
without relationship to Him brings the danger of twisting its meaning.

When Psalms tells us to hide the Word of God in our hearts, it means seeking the face of God for infusion—a life-giving infusion of the River of Life, the Bread of Heaven. It's not a magic formula, it's a relationship!

We can keep ourselves from deception, fear, and trauma by allowing the Lord to have total access to our minds and hearts. Knowing the Bible on the INSIDE of us is like a barometer that discerns the coming storms. The world is getting darker, so the Glory of God needs to be released in all of us to shine out to the world. Stand tall with love, respect and the Heart of God within you, and proclaim that Jesus Christ is Lord, to the Glory of God the Father. And keep the polish on that armor!

Love, Faye

Day Fifty-nine

"And let us consider one another in order to stir up love and
good works, not forsaking the assembling of ourselves together,
as is the manner of some, but exhorting one another,
and so much more as you see the Day approaching."

HEBREWS 10:24-25 NKJV

EXCERPT FROM *WALKING ON WITH JESUS*:

"Eliminate waste (hurt, fear, and all negatives). Replace it with love and faith-
fulness. Counteract the negative by the positive. Speak life. Be a proclaimer of
my peace. Establish my love. Surrounded by my angels, you shall go forth
unafraid. You have been established in my peace. You have been established in
my love. You have let go of the overwhelming forces of fear and rejection and
have looked to Me for your worth and abundance. I shall carry you forth with
ease and simplicity and it shall be known to My Glory that all is well with your
soul, for I have established it. Go forth with praise and thanksgiving and estab-
lish a trail for others to walk upon, proclaiming my goodness and love. My love
overshadows you and protects you and carries you forth into uncharted terri-
tory. Go forth without fear. Simply go forth in the security of my love. Strong,
immovable, and filled with my power are those who stand in my grace and
proclaim the divine providence and sustaining power of their God."

CLEANING THE CLOSET

In today's excerpt, we are encouraged to eliminate waste—the negatives, hurts, and fears. It's sort of like spring cleaning—digging out all
the old stained, torn clothing in our closets and throwing it all away. But
mostly, it's the stained junk clothes that have accumulated in the back of
the closet.

My closet sometimes has things that fall off the hangers and are
forgotten until I clean the closet out. Then I find a bunch of dusty, wrin-

kled old clothes that nobody should wear, including me, that need to be thrown away. And occasionally, they even contain spiders! Yikes!

Why should we care about what we say to people or how we say it? Because all of us (I speak from personal experience) are imperfect. (1 Corinthians 13:9.) What we hear in the Spirit realm can get filtered through our own minds and get messed up. As today's excerpt reminds us, it is the positive, encouraging Love of God that brings life! A clean heart gives us personal freedom and fearlessness, and faith rises up in our hearts, as well as in the hearts of those we touch!

In ministry, if we are trying to minister the Word and the Love of God (those need to be linked together) from a heart that is filled with the need to control, fears, rejection issues, or other religious stuff, we can hurt people instead of help them. These are the old clothes, the clothes of the flesh, not the Holy Spirit. In any meeting, such things cause people to feel unsafe. They don't want to return to the meeting, because they will continue to encounter the "old clothes from the floor in the back of the closet." In other words, the people who attend any meeting within the Body of Christ must honor and respect one another enough not to allow their own agendas to rear their ugly heads. The best way to do that is to clean out the closet!

Christian meetings should be safe places. Places where women and men can come and be refreshed by the Holy Spirit, which is necessary in these difficult times. So let's do some spring cleaning in the closets of our hearts, so that we don't push people away from places where they need to be. May we all be a safe place of refreshment!

Love, Faye

Day Sixty

"Oh, how great is Your goodness, which You have laid up for those who fear You, which You have prepared for those who trust in You in the presence of the sons of men! You shall hide them in the secret place of Your presence from the plots of man; You shall keep them secretly in pavilion from the strife of tongues. Blessed be the LORD, for He has shown me His marvelous kindness in a strong city."

PSALM 31:19-21 NKJV

EXCERPT FROM *WALKING ON WITH JESUS*:

"The passages of time clear the way for new beginnings and new openings in the Spirit. Time is your friend and brings forth the blessings spoken of. So many passages of time in the growth of a tree before it ever sets fruit. Even when it flowers, the flowers face and fall off, making way for the fruit. So it has been in your life. Lasting fruit takes time. Fear not because of time. It is your friend. Milestones along the way refresh and bring to mind my promises. Resist not the parameters of time. I say again, 'It is your friend.'"

HURRY UP, GOD! WHERE'S MY RESURRECTION?

If we were honest, we would confess that we are constantly telling God what to do, and that He should hurry up about it. I have often complained that God's wristwatch is not set to mine and He seems to do everything at the last minute. At least it's MY last minute. It is definitely not His.

As the Alpha and Omega, the Beginning and the End, our God's clock does not operate as ours does. He sees everything all at once, without the linear problem we have.

When Jesus walked among men, He knew from the beginning who He was and what His purpose on earth would be. He could see past the limitations of mankind to the end result (the joy that was set before Him). Because of His own death, He would receive the nations as His inheritance, and the people who accepted Him as His friends. His disciples didn't understand until the day of Pentecost. In fact until that day, their faith was shaken, their fears of the Romans and Jews off the charts, and they did not know if they would live. When Jesus was crucified, they came "under siege."

For centuries, one method of warfare was to "lay siege" to a city. Simply put, this strategy was to attack with such "shock and awe"— overwhelming force—that the people of the city would either all be killed or eventually collapse and give up. If you haven't noticed, most of the Christian people on earth are currently under siege. Illness, finances, relationships, distractions, governmental hostility, tribal hostility, false prophets, sin infiltrations, lost jobs, hatred and murder, church breakups, you name it, we've been in it. So we beg, yell, and jump up and down at the Lord to hurry up and help us.

God's timing, however, is absolutely perfect. Let me use a nice, safe example. One day I had to go out of town to see a friend who lives about 45 minutes away. While it had snowed and rained in those mountains, on the day I was traveling, the weather was partly cloudy and the roads totally clear. Had I waited until Friday, however, it would have been a different story. The roads that day were slick from another storm that passed through. And my little car isn't very good in slick conditions. God had the timing perfect, and my visit was joyous rather than marred by weather.

As today's excerpt claims, time really IS our friend. It is a place where God sets up circumstances and especially heart conditions that will bring about the best results. Sometimes we want what we want when we want it—but it's not the best timing for God to accomplish His purposes. So we wait. But make no mistake, God's Word stands, no matter what time we think it is. We just need to adjust our eyes to God's eyes, and our hearts to His heart: and stand in trust for the timing.

Jesus' death and resurrection changed not only history, but Heaven. Now we have access to heavenly time, and God's heart. We can snuggle into His wings and wait until the clock chimes that the time is here for us to receive or do things that have been promised. We don't have to worry about anything, because He is our refuge. Our resurrection, both in the spirit and in the natural, is sure and when it happens, all of Heaven will rejoice with us! No "siege" can stop the power of the Living God!

Love, Faye

Day Sixty-one

"If then you were raised with Christ, seek those things which
are above, where Christ is, sitting at the right hand of God.
Set your mind on things above, not on things on the earth.
For you died, and your life is hidden with Christ in God. When Christ,
who is our life appears, then you also will appear with Him in glory."

COLOSSIANS 3:1-4 NKJV

EXCERPT FROM *WALKING ON WITH JESUS*:

"Security in the world is fleeting. Security in Me lasts forever. Your heart has longed for security. Come up higher, my child. Cease from your striving and fall into my arms of love and security. You have known my heart as few do. Rest in my heart. Seek to respond to my slightest nudge. When you are resting in my arms, the slightest nudge seems strong and easily perceived. But when you are racing, even the strongest nudge can be missed. In My Presence, child, there is rest and clarity. Situations come and go, but make this your solid goal, to walk in Me in such a way as to never miss a word I say."

HIGHER IN HEAVENLY PLACES

Today's excerpt reminds us to "come up higher." Sometimes, when we are standing in front of an insurmountable, very difficult situation, that seems impossible. But God's Presence, knowing His security, will help us overcome by lifting us into heavenly places.

One day while in prayer, I saw a picture of a sheer cliff. It was slick, covered with slimy moss, and would not have been scalable by even the most experienced of mountain climbers. I was standing at the bottom of the cliff looking up at its impossible size, when I heard the Lord say, "Come up higher." Immediately, He took me high above the cliff and had me look down. You could not tell it was a cliff from that height! In fact, it looked like a little bump on the map! From 30,000 feet, for example, the Grand Canyon looks like a little ripple in the earth!

God's perspective on obstacles is not ours. We see things as obstacles when they are nothing more than pebbles along the path. So how do we come up higher? First, we should quiet the racing in our minds by thinking about the Lord. Once we have calmed down a bit, then we can ask Him to help us see from His perspective. Then He will give us "Hinds Feet in High Places" to navigate the situation.

What does that mean—"hinds feet in high places"? Hinds (or deer or other members of that animal group), do not perceive things as obstacles when they are in the direct path before them. My husband and I were driving slowly along a back road one day when out of nowhere, a herd of deer ran straight at us! They were focused on crossing the road, and even though our car was moving, they did not perceive us as an obstacle. They CLIMBED up and over our car and the car in front of us and ran off into the woods! Fortunately, we were going very slowly. The Lord reminded me at that point that faith in the security of His Presence will help us not perceive everything as a problem—we'll just go right over the top of it!

May the Lord grant us all the ability to perceive our situations as just bumps on the path—and may He give us the grace and power to climb over the top of them as if they weren't even a problem at all! And may we all cling closely to our Lord whatever we face.

Love, Faye

"He who dwells in the secret place of the Most High shall abide under the shadow of the Almighty. I will say of the LORD, 'He is my refuge and my fortress; My God, in Him I will trust.'"
—Psalm 91:1-2 NKJV

Day Sixty-two

"Then I answered and said to him, 'What are these two olive trees—
at the right of the lampstand, and at its left?' And I further answered
and said to him, 'What are these two olive branches that drip into the
receptacles of the two gold pipes from which the golden oil drains?'
Then he answered me and said, 'Do you not know what these are?'
And I said, 'No, my lord.'
So he said 'These are the two anointed ones,
who stand beside the Lord of the whole earth.'"

ZECHARIAH 4:11-14 NKJV

EXCERPT FROM *WALKING ON WITH JESUS*:

*"Know that I will always be there to meet you as you step forth, faithful in my
service. The Words of My Spirit will truly pour forth from you in abundance,
and the well will never run dry, but will always run clear, fresh, and unpolluted,
kept clean and pure by my love. Judge not that you be not judged, but give forth
a pure stream of my love."*

FRESH OIL

The first time I read the Scripture passage from Zechariah above, I
had a picture in my head of golden oil pouring out of the olive trees from
a spigot, a stream that only God could turn off. Bible scholars are fond
of saying that the "branches" are the same two prophets from
Revelation. But there is a picture for all of us in it!

The Bible is very clear that "oil" is a symbol of the indwelling Presence
of the Holy Spirit—the anointing, the Anointed One, the Presence of
God that flows from us. The River of Life is also that picture—the
Presence of the Holy Spirit that flows from us in power.

The passage in Zechariah, like the book excerpt from today, talks to
us about fresh oil, fresh water that comes forth, not used up, stagnant
flows. As long as we stay deeply and personally connected to God, we
are the "sons of fresh oil"—those who never move from the Presence of

the Lord. Some versions, like the King James, call it "anointed ones." Our freshness will never run dry for as long as we stay close to the Living God!

It is our responsibility, however, to make sure we are in the Presence of God, and not a stagnant or bitter stream. If what is flowing from us is stinky old oil, it will not produce the freshness God would have it bring! (As a natural example, have you ever cooked with used, stale oil? It ruins the taste of the food.)

The anointing of the Living God breaks yokes—in other words, it sets people free of the old ways and bondages that have been their patterns forever. All of us at some point have lived in bondage to something—food, image, alcohol, drugs, sex, television, materialism, religion, etc.—but the anointing of the Lord broke that off of us! We now can hear His Voice, and are able to be effective in whatever He asks us to do. His anointing is a faucet that, once we allow it to be turned on, becomes a stream, a source of life and hope for everyone around us!

The two "anointed ones" are a picture of us as those who stand close to the Lord. The olive trees full of fresh oil are a picture of our lives and our love for God. They will flourish as long as our roots grow deep into the Lord. As today's excerpt reminds us, we are a place from which a pure stream of God's love should flow!

Love, Faye

Day Sixty-two

"And we have known and believed the love that God has for us.
God is love, and he who abides in love abides in God,
and God in him…. There is no fear in love, but perfect love
casts out fear, because fear involves torment. But he who fears
has not been made perfect in love. We love Him,
because He first loved us."

1 JOHN 4:16,18-19 NKJV

EXCERPT FROM *WHEN GOD SPEAKS TO MY HEART*:

"Strong faith in Me is the key to walking victoriously. Struggles may come, but the strength of my voice commands the enemy to stop; and my triumph in your life is then made evident. Be strong in heart and mind through a firm commitment to listen for and obey that inner witness of my love toward you. Be encouraged this day to turn from the daily distractions that would steal your joy and instead, receive my hand of blessing. My favor is upon you and forever clears the way as you enter My Presence with praise and thanksgiving. The earth rejoices at the sound of one rejoicing in their King. We shall prevail together!"

THE INNER WITNESS OF GOD'S LOVE

The most important gift that a person can receive is the inner witness of God's love in their life. It is an anchor which will protect them in every situation, and will cause them to follow God's voice no matter what their circumstances may be. Without it, old thoughts and pressures can creep in and destroy us.

I once had a friend and coworker who had a very poor self-image. Although she had met Jesus at one point in her life, the enemy constantly reminded her of her failures. He barraged her with negative thoughts toward herself. She started drinking to cope. Eventually she became an alcoholic, and ultimately died of cirrhosis of the liver.

My Christian friends and I had spent hours and hours trying to help our friend understand how valuable she was to God. But the enemy had convinced her that she was worthless anyway, so why try. Her family also fed that negative thought process by telling her that she was a "loser." Her "inner witness" was silenced by lies straight from the pit.

After my friend's funeral, I was approached by her mother, who thanked me for being so nice to her "loser" daughter. Let's just say, after about a 5-minute conversation, her mother burst into tears with the realization that she had never known the real woman beneath the bad self-image.

God's love for us is total — He loves us no matter how many times we have failed. He loves us in spite of ourselves. He died on the cross BECAUSE we failed! He gave His love freely, simply because He cares about us and wants us as His friends. And all we have to do is accept it, draw close to Him, and allow His love to remove all that the past has done to bring us down. We will never be perfect, but His Perfection, His love, will keep us in all things.

Father, may Your Holy Spirit fill each one today with Your love, and let Him rise up and bring the witness of that love to all. Lord, drown out the negative voices that cover those with heartaches, lift up their hearts, and open their ears to hear Your wonderful voice!

Love, Faye

Day Sixty-three

"Give us this day our daily bread.
And forgive us our debts, as we forgive our debtors."

MATTHEW 6:11-12 NKJV

EXCERPT FROM *WALKING ON WITH JESUS*:

"Circumstances are moments in time. Don't let them control whole segments of time in your thought life. Give others grace as I give you grace. Stealing from yesterday (pulling from yesterday's circumstances) wreaks havoc with today. Grace is given for today's circumstances, not yesterday's. Leave yesterday behind and live today, unhindered by yesterday and unencumbered by tomorrow. There is only grace for today and its blessings. That is how you can love each person you come in contact with unreservedly. Leave the past behind and live totally in the present, rejoicing in the blessings and benefits therein. Cancel old debts and mark them paid!"

CANCEL THE DEBT!

It's hard for me to believe on a daily basis how many problems Christians have with each other! We are easily offended, carry animosity for years, and complain about one another at the drop of a hat. We think we are better than everyone else. (Note: there is a difference between "processing" difficult situations by talking about them, and deliberately being hard about something.)

In the 80's, a couple of my closest friends deliberately fell into sin, lied to me about it, and then became hostile. They weren't babies in Christ; they knew fully what they were doing. I was devastated. I was angry. I nurtured a bitterness seed for years. Did it help? No. I couldn't focus on the Lord. I spent most of my time thinking about how my friends had hurt me and how God should punish them.

What I didn't understand was that sin carries its own punishment, and that is sufficient without my input. All I did was try to pull "yesterday" along with me—and it wasted five years of my life.

Today's excerpt may seem basic, but the vast majority of the Body of Christ does not walk in it. Today let us stop and from the bottom of our hearts, not only forgive one another (truly forgive, not lip service), but cancel the anger that our brothers and sisters may have caused. If we are involved in a situation, no matter whose fault it may have been, let go of the animosity and drop the debts owed to us. We must accept that place of forgiveness and forget the wrongs. God gives us grace, so we must grant grace to others.

In the situation I mentioned above, I learned several years later of the suffering my friends went through because of their choices. But our God worked it out to their good. Today they are mighty, powerful servants of God, with His praises on their lips and a focus entirely on Him. Our relationships are totally restored, and "all debts cancelled" between us. We are in a place of trust and friendship, forged by the forgiveness of Christ. I've learned a lesson in how to let go of things that hurt us. Let's all live today unhindered by yesterday, and unencumbered by tomorrow. Fear and anger cannot live where love and forgiveness reign!

Love, Faye

Day Sixty-four

"A father of the fatherless and a judge and protector of widows
is God in His holy habitation. God places the solitary in
families and gives the desolate a home in which to dwell;
He leads the prisoners out to prosperity;
but the rebellious dwell in a parched land."

PSALM 68:5-6 AMP

EXCERPT FROM *WALKING ON WITH JESUS*:

"The days and years have come and come, but they've left within your heart my song. Let it ring within your heart. Let it heal the festering darts from trials past, bringing forth healing that will last. Within your heart, the answer is given to those who know not how to keep on living. Songs of hope, love, and faith, to lift their hearts and make them feel safe in their Father's arms, safe from harm."

SAFE IN THE FATHER'S ARMS

Did you see in today's Scripture and excerpt the heart of God? God is the Father of the fatherless, the judge and protector of the widows in His holy habitation. His holy habitation is US!

When I was a child, I loved the times when I could sit in my Daddy's lap and feel his arms around me. While Daddy was my imperfect earthly father, his love for me was obvious and real. Many times, he stood against people who tried to take advantage of me or hurt me. He demonstrated his protection and love by his actions.

Many of us in the Body of Christ have an opposite view of fathers. Many had no love growing up, many had no father at all. But all of us are called to allow our Heavenly Father to dwell in our hearts in a way that releases Him to protect and love others.

God gives all of us that gift of being a protector, a righteous judge of right and wrong (not judgmental religiosity), and the ability to bring a person safe into their Heavenly Father's arms. This requires faith; it requires a love of God deep from within our hearts. If we do not love, we cannot touch the lives of others with His refuge of safety (1 John 4).

May you know today the feeling of warmth and safety that exists in the arms of the Lord. May you know that He is the Father who loves you, even if you had no love of a father as a child. You are His beloved!

Love, Faye

Day Sixty-five

"For the earnest expectation of the creation eagerly awaits for the revealing of the sons of God. For the creation was subjected to futility, not willingly, but because of Him who subjected it in hope; because creation itself also will be delivered from the bondage of corruption into the glorious liberty of the children of God."

ROMANS 8:19-21 NKJV

EXCERPT FROM *WHEN GOD SPEAKS TO MY HEART*:

"Teach others to be still and know Me with an assurance of my love and care. Strengthen the hearts and hands around you. Be a lighthouse of hope and freedom in such a way as to say, 'You can do what He has created you to do and be.' My love will set them free. My love is security. I will fulfill the need and bless, providing every day. My matchless love is the only way. Be my love, my child!"

THE REVEALING OF THE SONS OF GOD

There aren't many things as lovely as spring, when the flowers and trees begin to shed their death and reveal fresh new life in the blossoms and buds that come out. But there is another fresh new life spoken of in Scripture that is even more exciting: the revealing of the sons of God. "Sons," or *huios*, in today's Scripture passage means the mature offspring, the ones who have grown up and are ready for their inheritance. They know how to let God be preeminent, instead of themselves.

Remember the items that were placed in the Ark of the Covenant? The Ark was the very embodiment of the Presence of God in Israel. It contained His Word, His Power, and His Provision. In symbolic terms, it contained the picture of Jesus Christ, the Son of God.

Word: Jesus is the *Logos*, the Word, the actual manifestation of God's Glory and the fulfillment of the Law. The tablets of stone given to Moses (the Law) were placed in the Ark.

Power: Jesus showed in action the giving of miracles and healing. God sent us the Holy Spirit to continue that work. The Ark contained Aaron's rod that budded. It was a dead stick that came to life, just as Jesus himself rose from the dead!

Provision: The Jews were fed with manna, the bread of heaven. As Jesus reminded His hearers that He is the Bread that came down from Heaven, so the manna placed in the Ark was there to remind us of Jesus' place as the bread of life. He IS our provision for all things, and in all of those things is His perfect Love manifest!

As the temple of God once contained the Ark of His Presence, we now as the temple should contain His Presence! There is coming a day in which the temple of God will be opened in heaven, and His Ark will be seen in His temple (Revelation 11:19). It will be a day of revelation of the sons of God, amidst the mighty power of the Living God.

As today's excerpt reminds us, we must know that we can do and be what He has required of us. We must have faith and walk in His Love and Presence, and grow up into mature heirs who will do as He says. That day is a certainty. Even the earth is waiting for it! Yes, Lord!

Love, Faye

Day Sixty-six

"…And after the earthquake a fire, but the LORD was not in the fire; and after the fire a still, small, voice."

1 KINGS 19:12 NKJV

EXCERPT FROM *WALKING ON WITH JESUS*:

"Your Father, who has created you for this day and for this moment, has spoken forth the creative word, 'Come forth!' Be all that I have created you to be. Do all that I have created you to do. See all I have created you to see. My Spirit calls you forth this day! Bright are the days ahead, filled with adventure and light. Mighty are the days ahead that have been born out of struggle to stand. Standing has been my plan for you through the years. It has been the formation of what you see and know. Standing is never easy. It is wearisome, but the rewards are great. Be encouraged this day as you continue to stand in My Presence with faith, hope, and love."

OUT OF THE CAVE

Elijah was in a really bad situation. He had just hit the pinnacle of his career as a prophet by proving the false gods were worthless, and prophesying the end of a long drought. So, of course, his enemies threatened to kill him. Help! He went into a cave on Mount Horeb to hide in frustration, and whined loudly at the Lord for the situation (1 Kings 19). We'd never do that, would we?

The Lord told Elijah to go and stand before Him. A huge wind came up and smashed the rocks around Elijah. God wasn't there. Then a huge earthquake struck and shook everything…still no God. Then a fire tore through the countryside in front of him. God did not appear. But, didn't God ask him to go there? Wasn't God going to exact revenge on his enemies right then? Where was the immediate answer to Elijah's complaint? It came as Elijah stood, when the silence came, and he opened his ears to hear God's "still, small voice." God softly beckoned him to the mouth of the cave and asked him what he was doing there. And then Elijah repeated his complaint. Instead of deliverance or immediate answer, the Lord sent Elijah back to anoint new people for the finishing of the task. But he had to get out of the cave to do it.

In today's excerpt, we find that God is calling us out to be and do and see. If we are waiting for the lightning bolt in our front yard for a sign, that's not where it will be. It will be in the still, small voice. And sometimes it takes having to go through the fires of life to prepare us for the day when we can actually hear that voice over our own agendas.

We are in a pivotal point in history, not only for the world, but for the Kingdom of God. We can stay in the cave and miss it, or we can hear His Voice and step outside to finish our destiny. Many have been rejected, many have suffered frustrating setbacks, but it is time to move those aside, crush the fear that rises up, and move forward. Out of the cave! God is calling you forth!

Love, Faye

Day Sixty-seven

"But I will hope continually, and will praise You yet more and more.
My mouth shall tell of Your righteous acts and of Your deeds of
salvation all the day, for their number is more than I know.
I will come in the strength and mighty acts of the Lord God;
I will mention and praise Your righteousness, even Yours alone."
PSALM 71:14-16 AMP

EXCERPT FROM *WHEN GOD SPEAKS TO MY HEART*:

"The scenery is changing, my child, along your pathway chosen by Me. A new path is ahead—a place of beauty, peace, and fellowship with Me. Once again you will come to a new day full of hope and excitement. For now, continue to bathe in the wonderment and beauty of this appointed time of quiet in My Presence. Let Me take care of the rest of your life. It is safe in my hands and shall come forth to your joy and to my glory. Rejoice in the now, in the magnitude and absolute beauty of all I have created for your life. I treasure this time with you!"

THE RIDE OF OUR LIVES

Whenever the Lord tells us that the "scenery is changing," we can be certain that the ride of our lives is coming. The challenge is to take it with faith in the "Driver" and not freak out along the way!

My husband, Myron, is a case in point. For several summers, we visited San Francisco. Now, he is an excellent driver, the product of years of experience, but he takes great delight in teasing me. San Francisco, as some of you may know, is built on steep hills that have what I call "bumps" along the way. Myron likes to take back streets a little faster than I'd like, just to see me squirm. So as we drove downhill, occasionally we'd "catch air"—and I would occasionally scream. And of course, my knuckles were clutching the dashboard until they turned white. He was not driving over the speed limit, nor was he doing anything illegal—I just don't like to drive fast downhill. He snickered and took me out to dinner to calm me down. I love him. And it's a good thing I know he's a good driver!

In our pathways with the Lord, there are always times when His chosen route takes us on an uncomfortable ride. He does that to stretch us, to work our faith muscles in ways that help us to learn that He has never left us, in spite of the discomfort of new scenery and different experiences.

The number of God's righteous acts is not known to us. We just have to trust that no matter what pathway we are traversing, His love will see us through it to a better place. We will know Him better. We will see Him work great things. We will learn to trust His "driving" in our lives. And above all, His Love and Presence will change our hearts along the way!

Love, Faye

Day Sixty-eight

"But none of these things move me; nor do I count my life
dear to myself, so that I may finish my race with joy,
and the ministry which I received from the Lord Jesus,
to testify to the gospel of the grace of God."

ACTS 20:24 NKJV

EXCERPT FROM *WALKING ON WITH JESUS*:

*"Do not let misgivings cause you to stray from your course. Remember my
blessings, promises, and teachings. The Spirit of the Lord shall go before you
and multiply your conquests and victories. Stick to the high road of my calling.
Measure and weigh the results with my promises. You shall be pleased and lives
shall be blessed."*

THE RIGHT RUNNING SHOES

There is a 7K race the first Sunday in May in Spokane, Washington,
called "Bloomsday." It's a pretty big event for our area, with thousands
of competitors from all over the world. It is also a challenge for those
non-athletic folks who enjoy that first blush of spring exercise. When I
was younger and in better shape, I gave it a shot.

The first lesson the Lord taught me was that those who tried to actually run in flip-flops, dress shoes, or barefoot had a problem by the time
they were halfway through the race: blisters and excruciating pain
slowed them down. A friend had signed up with me to run, but by the
time the race was over, he was a long way back in the pack. He had worn
men's dress shoes. His feet were covered in blisters by the finish line!

Those of us who had good shoes were tired and achy, but we didn't
have excruciating pain, and we were able to reach the finish line without
major problems. We finished our race with joy.

The Bible says that we are to have our feet shod with the preparation of the gospel of peace (Ephesians 6:15). Today's excerpt reminds us

to remember God's promises, teachings, and blessings. THAT is preparation—knowing Jesus! He is the very embodiment of the "gospel of peace." If we know what He said to us (His Word) and if we know Him, we can make sure the way we walk is sound and sure (that we are wearing the "right shoes"). This is the way to stop distractions that would take us off the course.

If you are wearing God's brand of shoes, you can rest assured that your calling and destiny is certain. The race course will be clearly marked, and He will help you stay on it. May God's peace be with you today as you run the race, knowing that He has gone before you to smooth the road!

Love, Faye

Day Sixty-eight

"Though an army may encamp against me, my heart shall not fear;
though war may rise against me, in this I will be confident.
One thing I have desired of the LORD, that will I seek: that I may
dwell in the house of the LORD all the days of my life, to behold the
beauty of the LORD, and to inquire in His temple. For in the time of
trouble He shall hide me in His pavilion; in the secret place of His
tabernacle He shall hide me; He shall set me high upon a rock."

PSALM 27:3-5 NKJV

EXCERPT FROM *WALKING ON WITH JESUS*:

"Strong and sturdy I have made you, able to bear up under the constant barrage
that threatened to undo you. Should you say, 'My God has forsaken me?' No,
I say to you! Go forth unafraid and able to say, 'My God reigns! Nothing can
get past His ability to bring victory!' Stand fast! Stand firm and stand strong!
Say to the mountain, 'Be cast into the sea!' Say to your heart, 'The victory is
the Lord's!'"

SHADOW BOXING

One night after worship at a meeting, I and two ladies had a wonderful, joyful few minutes talking and laughing about some embarrassing moments. It occurred to me that some of our hysterically funny experiences were caused by sheer fear—we had been shadow boxing: fighting an enemy that could not harm us.

In Psalm 23, David reminds us that the valley is a SHADOW of death. For the believer, death is not the end, but the beginning. But what about normal every day things? How do we navigate the smaller things that trip us up?

One night when I was in high school, I went up the hill to a neighbor's home to visit at about dusk. By the time I went home, it was pitch black out, with a full moon that cast eerie shadows over the path. And, wouldn't you know, we had just watched a scary movie. Out of the corner of my eye, a shadow moved and I lost it. I froze and started screaming so loudly that the entire neighborhood showed up. My cousin slapped me to get me back to reality. And then I felt VERY stupid. I had been fearful of something that was not real.

God has promised us an abundant life (John 10:10). He says that we will never lack (Psalm 23). He says that we'll even be more beautiful than the sparrows and flowers (Matthew 6:26-34). Thing is, do we really believe it? When the checking account is empty, what do we do? When you can't get your car fixed, or the plumbing is leaking into the basement, or there's no money to replace the torn clothing in your closet, how do you not fear?

The absolute only way to navigate these shadows of disaster with faith is to remind ourselves about what the Lord says. We can't work it up, make it up, or fix it up on our own. We need the Holy Spirit's gift of faith for everything we encounter. We may have to remind ourselves through clenched teeth. We may have to grab a box of tissue as we stand on His Word, but we can overcome any attack with the knowledge that He will never forsake us.

Fear, as the Bible reminds us, involves torment. We have fear when we think something bad is going to happen to us, and God isn't going to help us. But just the opposite is true: He will help us in EVERY situation. In war, in peace, against all odds, our God loves us and sets our feet on a rock. I don't know about you, but that's why I will serve Him forever. Fear is a shadow, a threat of harm that cannot touch us—no more shadow boxing! Praise to our God is the answer!

Love, Faye

Day Sixty-nine

"Behold, God is my salvation, I will trust and not be afraid.
For YAH, the LORD is my strength and song; He has also
become my salvation. Therefore with joy you will draw
water from the wells of salvation. And in that day you will say:
'Praise the LORD, call upon His name; declare His deeds
among the peoples, make mention that His name is exalted.'"

ISAIAH 12:2-4 NKJV

EXCERPT FROM *WALKING ON WITH JESUS*:

"The gate has been swung wide open for you. Pitch a tent in the wilderness, that you can continue to go in and out and minister to the needs of those who are still in the wilderness, hungering and thirsting for the Word of Life that will set them free. You shall show others that there is a way through the wilderness that leads to life, refreshing, and hope. I will show you how to minister hope to a dying people with no hope. You are a picture story and My Spirit is upon you to bring forth my will and abundant life, full and free. Let not your heart be troubled, neither let it be afraid, for my hand of restoration and freedom is upon you, and the reality of my love shall be manifest and made known to you in a new and all inclusive way. In peace you shall drink from the well of restoration. Your soul shall magnify the Lord and recount His mercies to you and you shall see and respond to new ways of moving by My Spirit of truth."

THE WELL OF RESTORATION

Y'shuwah—salvation. In today's scripture, the word *Y'shuwah* is used several times. It means help, deliverance, victory, welfare, safety, ease. It has the connotation for good health, prosperity, comfort, and rescue from trouble. In those promises we find restoration, because Y'shuwah is His Name—Jesus!

In the seasons of our lives, we often end up in the wilderness, and have lost nearly everything. Case in point: when I was very young in the

Lord, I went through a nasty breakup of a relationship which caused me to be in grinding poverty for a long time. I stood in discount grocery stores with my $7 per week for food, with tears welling up in my eyes, and found a way to eat in spite of the tiny amount of money available. It was a heart-breaking time in the wilderness.

Our God is faithful. To that I can attest with every ounce of my being. I made it through those difficult years, and God granted me the joy of salvation. He restored my life and the hope in my heart!

Wells in the Bible are places where life-giving water is found. Many of these wells were found in deserts where intense heat punishes the weary. Today, if you are in a place where circumstances are overwhelming you and thirst for relief consumes your heart, lift your face toward God and hear His Voice remind you that a well of restoration, a well of salvation has been dug for you!

As long as we live on the earth, deserts will come and go. The wilderness experience can sometimes be our fault, but as was the case with Joshua and Caleb, sometimes it's the fault of others. As long as we hold fast to the Living God, we can show people where His wells are dug, and encourage one another as we travel out of the desert. His Presence, His Holy Spirit will never leave us no matter how hot the experience gets. He is the God whose name is Salvation, and every ounce of His being is Love. Joy is found in that well! Come and drink!

Love, Faye

Day Seventy

"But the Lord stood with me and strengthened me, so that
the message might be preached fully through me, and that all the
Gentiles might hear. Also I was delivered out of the mouth of the lion.
And the Lord will deliver me from every evil work and preserve me for
His heavenly kingdom. To Him be glory forever and ever. Amen!"

2 TIMOTHY 4:17-18 NKJV

EXCERPT FROM *THE SINGING BRIDE*:

*"As I reveal My Master Plan to you, receive it with open arms and rebuke the
enemy as he comes to cover up the Master Plan and relocate your focus. But My
Master Plan shall go forth unabated and it shall open doors that I have preordained from the foundation of the world. And you shall walk through those
doors and you shall see my face as you have never seen it before. And you shall
radiate My Glory as you never have radiated it before. And you shall go forth in
my freedom and my foundations that have been built within your life shall not
fail you. They shall be strong and secure, and nations shall know of my love
through your voice and through your heart reaching out to them. So receive,
receive, receive and know this, my child, that nothing shall miss its mark and
nothing that I have proclaimed by My Word shall fail to come to pass."*

THE LION'S DEN

We all live in a lion's den right now, one that contains "lions" who are
being starved into hatred, anger, and vengeance. But it might be helpful
to remember this about lions in the natural: the dominant adult male is
the absolute ruler of the pride. Absolute. That means that all who try to
usurp his authority might as well not bother. No offspring of another
male are tolerated, no compromise is allowed in his arena. Even though
the lioness' are the hunters, he is the ruler!

God is our Absolute Protector. He surrounds us with an ever-vigi-
lant angelic host. He covers us with His wings and His love. If anyone
tries to take us away from Him, they will fail. If they turn up the flames,

He will appear in the flames with us. If they throw us into the lion's den, we will curl up and sleep safely among them. The roar of our Lord God over us is the signal to the enemy of our souls that he might as well not bother unless he wants a fight that he will lose. We belong to the Lord!

In today's excerpt and Scripture, God declares that the way has been paved for us. It is HIS way, His plan, His protection. He opens doors, and no mere man can stop His purposes. No demon can stand in the way. They can "roar," but their sound is very puny compared to God. He is the Lion of the Tribe of Judah and we carry Him in our hearts. No weapon formed against us shall prosper!

Love, Faye

Day Seventy-one

"As the Father knows Me, even so I know the Father; and I lay down
My life for the sheep. And other sheep I have which are not of this
fold; them also I must bring, and they will hear My voice; and there
will be one flock and one shepherd. Therefore My Father loves Me,
because I lay down My life that I may take it again."

JOHN 10:15-17 NKJV

EXCERPT FROM *WHEN GOD SPEAKS TO MY HEART*:

*"My child, walk in your life—freely. Live a life of abundance. Stand back,
survey, and forgive. It is a testament of My Spirit residing and acting in you.
Daily cleanse your heart of all the built-up debris. Don't allow the day to pile
up, surround, and overpower you. Discard it all. Go forth this day, determined
to be my clear channel of love, free from all bondage. Lay down your life before
Me. Minister life to those around you! Build up their hearts, and they shall see
the glory of their God. Walk in my goodness, live freely, and be unencumbered.
You are precious to Me!"*

LIE DOWN

Today's excerpt has a statement that is often used as a religious tool
to force us all into submission. "Lay down your life before Me." What
does that mean? It's actually pretty simple: follow the principle set forth
by Jesus. Don't get all wound up in form or legalism, just be the love of
God to others and it will come naturally.

Speaking from personal experience, it's easy to be so stressed and
upset by what other people say or do to us, that we can become mean
rather than show the love of God to them. A case in point: one night I
was baking homemade bread and was up to my elbows in bread dough.
The phone rang. I answered it, but heard nothing on the other end so I
hung up. I no more than got my hands back in the dough, when the
phone rang again. As this scenario played out two more times, I got mad.
When it rang again, I lost it and shouted a four-letter word into the

phone and slammed the receiver down. Did I pray first? Was I calm? No, not a chance. As I slammed the phone down, I realized the phone company needed to be notified, so I hiked down to my office and notified them. They fixed the problem right away.

Why did I respond that way? Because someone annoyed ME. Someone inconvenienced ME. It was all about ME. ME, I, MINE: words that prove we have not laid our lives before God!

When the phone rang again, this time someone responded. The previous calls were from my Pastor. He had just finished telling the operator that this was an emergency and I was one of his parishioners. All she heard was the bad language and anger. Pretty poor testimony!

Over the years I have learned that sometimes situations need a firm, but gentle response. While I am a work in progress, I am learning that laying down my life means removing my own personal opinions, judgments, and feelings from a situation. When someone does something annoying to me, the best response is firm but loving, or sometimes I need to let it go with forgiveness entirely. Having a heart that understands the suffering of others will bring the people to you who need Jesus the most. Those who hurt us are in worse shape than we are, and need the love of Christ. Those who annoy, pick on, hate, or even try to harm us are those who need Jesus. OUR RESPONSE makes the difference for them.

Jesus laid aside His tallit, His garments, to wash the feet of His disciples (John 13:4). He laid aside that which was precious to Him, the things that covered Him from exposure to others, in order to serve. He laid down His life for us to access relationship to the Father. He laid down His Divinity to share common ground with the downtrodden and broken. Can we lay down our junk, moment by moment, to share a touch of love, kindness, and patience with others?

Love, Faye

Day Seventy-two

"Let all bitterness, wrath, anger, clamor, and evil speaking be put away
from you, with all malice. And be kind to one another, tenderhearted,
forgiving one another, just as God in Christ also forgave you."

EPHESIANS 4:31-32 NKJV

EXCERPT FROM *WHEN GOD SPEAKS TO MY HEART*:

*"My child, put your trust in Me. If you have done wrong, repent and go on.
Forgiveness brings life. Repent and rejoice in Me. Lighten your burden by
giving it to Me. Don't carry that which was not meant to be carried. If you have
been hurt, give it to Me. Then, go on your way rejoicing. Love with your whole
heart, free from concern, and turn the other cheek. Anger cannot feed in such an
environment. It can feed upon itself but not upon you. Keep your spirit pure
before Me. Do not give anger or bitterness a moment to breed."*

THE TREE THAT GROWS IN OUR HEARTS

The Bible is filled with references to trees. Some of my favorites are
Psalm 1:2-3, Revelation 22:2, and Mark 4:31. The Lord loves to remind
us that what grows in us becomes the fruit of our lives. When we feed
His principles to our hearts and minds, we grow a giant strong tree of
life. When we don't, we do the opposite.

An example: recently in the news, a woman who had spent most of
her life as a single mom in an ordinary lifestyle became a terrorist, plot-
ting and desiring to be a suicide bomber. How could that happen? She
allowed bitterness to take root in her life, and it grew into a giant tree of
hatred—and it all started with her response to the things that went
wrong in her life.

Today's Scripture and excerpt are extremely important—while we
tend to think of them as abstract ideas, they are really very practical
tools to navigate through life's ups and downs.

A few years ago, my earthly father passed away from heart failure. He had promised me all of my life that he had made provision for my future in his estate. The hitch was that he made someone else the executor, and used a non-binding type of will that is not overseen by a court. So when the time came, both my brother and I received nothing from the estate, and legally we had no recourse. At that point I had a choice: I could be bitter, angry, and hate that relative, or I could release it to the Lord and rely on Him. I could "turn the other cheek" and be planted in the Lord, or I could feed the bitterness tree. I chose to forget about it and love anyway. Recently I contacted that branch of the family and didn't mention anything—I just listened to their pain and blessed them. They were amazed, and we parted on a good note. God's love was the most important seed to plant in their lives.

In Mark 4:31, Jesus told the parable about a mustard seed that starts out so tiny you can almost not see it, but grows into a huge plant that becomes a resting place for birds. God asks us to refuse the things which will grow bad crops. He asks us to "turn the other cheek." It's not an admonition to become a rug, or to allow people to run over us with impunity. But it is a reminder to refuse those feelings which can change our hearts from purity to hatred in the blink of an eye. I don't know about you, but my heart wants to be a forest of God's trees and herbs, places where people and creatures alike may find rest and fresh food. How about you?

Love, Faye

Day Seventy-three

"Come to Me, all you who labor and are heavy laden, and I will give
you rest. Take My yoke upon you and learn from Me, for I am
gentle and lowly in heart, and you will find rest for your souls.
For My yoke is easy and My burden is light."
MATTHEW 11:28-30 NKJV

EXCERPT FROM ROSALIE'S JOURNAL:

*"My child, lean into my arms and commit your whole being unto Me. That is
called 'rest.' Rest from the fear of things left undone. Rest from the fear of
'missing it.' Rest from the clamoring to be.' For My Spirit in and through you
is all in all. Rest, my child, in Me, completely removed from the passing scene.
My Presence shall become precious to you in new ways undreamed of. Be
content in Me. Release unto Me all cares and worries. My hand is over you to
prepare you for what is to come. (It's being in the womb of God, being fashioned by His own hand of protection and creation. What a wonderful place to
be.) Secure in my hand, nothing can cause harm or interrupt my plan. Relax in
my hand and lean on Me with confidence and trust. All shall be accomplished
in my time and at my pace. Rest in Me, child. Be at peace and know Me. Be
saturated in my love. Tranquility of heart shall be the fruit. Nothing shall push
nor pull you in any direction but mine."*

RESTING IN THE FLAMES OF ADVERSITY

Truth be told, most of us are really awful at resting in the Lord, especially when the circumstances around us are driving us crazy. Our
instincts are to try and control the circumstances, and we will fight tooth
and nail to accomplish it...until the very reins of reality are stripped
from our hands. Then we are faced with the choice to rest or struggle.

One of the most wonderful gifts of our relationship to the Creator of
the Universe is rest. We don't hear much about it, but it came as the
package deal when we came to Christ. God rested on the seventh day of

creation, because creation was finished. When Jesus died on the cross, He spoke "It is finished." WE are part of that finish—the day when God himself stepped in, forgave us, and allowed us access to His Presence. It is a place of REST.

The four gospels—Matthew, Mark, Luke, John—have a lot of reminders to rest and have faith. In the boat on Galilee during the storm, the disciples should have rested, but they freaked out instead, so Jesus had to rebuke the storm. When it seemed as if there was no food for a large crowd, Jesus fed the crowd from two loaves of bread and a fish, and later had to scold the disciples to remember it.

There is a difference between struggling in God and resting. Resting does not mean ignoring situations or doing nothing. It DOES mean to cease from our soulish fighting and trust the Holy Spirit to run things. It is a cooperation between us and God, not a struggle to make things happen. One brings exhaustion, fear, and weariness, the other brings grace, peace, and fresh life. May you find the rest of God—the finished place of His love and Presence where you cease your struggles and let Him take the burden. Rest!

Love, Faye

Day Seventy-four

"Bless (affectionately, gratefully praise) the Lord, O my soul, and forget not [one of] all His benefits—Who forgives [every one of] all your iniquities, Who heals [each one of] all your diseases, Who redeems your life from the pit and corruption, Who beautifies, dignifies and crowns you with loving-kindness and tender mercy; Who satisfies your mouth [your necessity and desire at your personal age and situation] with good so that your youth, renewed, is like the eagle's [strong, overcoming, soaring]!"

PSALM 103:2-5 AMP

EXCERPT FROM ROSALIE'S JOURNAL:

"Be satisfied with who you are, where you're at and where you're going, knowing that I hold all things in my hands. Your growth is in my hands and all it requires is a willing and dedicated heart, walking with my faith and my love, moved along with my joy. A joyful heart is a peaceful heart, filled with trust and love, motivated by a desire to walk in my righteousness, not your own. Fulfillment and trust walk hand in hand. Trust in my mighty hand to move in your behalf. Have faith and win."

SATISFACTION GUARANTEED

The word "satisfy" is defined in English dictionaries as "fulfillment of desires, expectations, needs, wants." It brings an end to need. It gives assurance, and solves doubt. In the biblical sense, it denotes filled so much that it is satiated—completely watered until it overflows. If we fill a sponge with water and don't wring it out, it gets so full that it can't take in any more, and the water simply runs out of the sponge. THAT's biblical satisfaction: that we are so watered by God that the excess flows out of us in a mighty River of Life to others!

Now, since we live on the earth, we are subject to its problems. We always encounter challenges that threaten to dry us out. The children of Israel did not wander in the desert as God's perfect will; they wandered there because they lacked faith. We need the kind of trust and faith that pleases the Lord daily—it will keep us satisfied, filled up, full of His Glory!

Today's excerpt reminds us to trust in God's plan for us, no matter what we see around us. God will get us through, and use everything as a stepping stone in our lives. In my own life, I've had to take steps forward when it seemed as though those steps would destroy me. Yet, God had a plan, His love covered me, His strength carried me, and I came out fine.

It's not always easy to stay in that frame of mind—frequently we want or need so much that, like Moses, we start smacking the rock in a temper tantrum instead of obeying our God's instructions carefully. Sometimes I can envision the Lord's angels standing in my home, turning their backs and whispering to each other, "She's at it again. If we just wait, she'll shut up and we'll get this plan moving."

Faith requires one basic reminder: God is God, He is way smarter, bigger, and better at what He does than we are. All we have to do is trust Him. Not always easy, but always necessary. (Isaiah 55, Hebrews 11.)

Today may you know His benefits, His love, His Presence, and His power. May you find a new level of trust and faith. And may you be satisfied with the goodness of the Lord until you spill over and splash the world around you with His love!

Love, Faye

Day Seventy-five

"We can make a large horse go wherever we want by means of a small bit in its mouth. And a small rudder makes a huge ship turn wherever the pilot chooses to go, even though the winds are strong. In the same way, the tongue is a small thing that makes grand speeches. But a tiny spark can set a great forest on fire and the tongue is a flame of fire. It is a whole world of wickedness, corrupting your entire body. It can set your whole life on fire, for it is set on fire by hell itself."

JAMES 3:3-6 NLT

EXCERPT FROM ROSALIE'S JOURNAL:

"Stand forth strong in the strength of your Redeemer. Stand forth strong in the love of your Lord. Come forth in victory and praise. Come forth into the sunlight of my smile, refreshed, released, and restored, complete in every way. Bring forth unto Me glorious praise every day. Lift up to the Heavens your songs of praise. It will create an atmosphere of healing."

A CHANGE IN THE ATMOSPHERE

Proverbs 18:21 tells us that death and life are in the power of the tongue. Today's Scripture tells us that the tongue can destroy like a forest fire. And today's excerpt reminds us that praise to God can change the atmosphere and bring healing into any situation!

One of the most difficult principles to get through to people is that WE have the power to change the atmosphere wherever we go. It's very easy to get wound up in a situation and go negative—it's their fault, they're awful, the darkness is thick, blah blah blah. But WE are the carriers of the Living God—and He is the Light of the world! We can push back the darkness by the way we choose to relate to others, and what we do with our tongues.

Look at it this way: the law measures sin and death. It's like a thick blanket of judgment/performance that no one can live up to. The law is over everyone who does not know the Lord and who fails to walk in His love for others. But those who choose to show His attributes (Galatians 5:22) are not under the law, they are free! The heaviness of the law can't cover them, and the law can't judge them! So if we dwell in that place of God's love, we literally change the atmosphere around us by bringing freedom to it!

If we encounter people who are crusty and mean, the Word says to bless them. If we pray for those who hate us, then we literally change their destiny. I spoke with a friend this morning who inherited a gay employee in their new business. God has given her a tremendous love for this man who needs Jesus. He expected to be fired. He expected a destructive tirade of hate-language from her. He got love instead. She has literally set him on a new course, a new destiny. Instead of pushing him further toward hell, she has chosen to turn his head toward the love of the Father. He is changing, she is changing. And God is pushing back the darkness!

Today let's all be thankful for the love God has given to us, so that we can give it to others! Let's change the atmosphere with praises on our lips and the love of the Lord in our hearts!

Love, Faye

Day Seventy-six

"In the beginning God created the heavens and the earth.
The earth was formless and empty, and darkness covered the
deep waters. And the Spirit of God was hovering over the surface of
the waters. Then God said, 'Let there be light,' and there was light.
And God saw that the light was good. Then He separated the light
from the darkness. God called the light 'day' and the darkness 'night.'"

GENESIS 1:1-5 NLT

EXCERPT FROM *WALKING ON WITH JESUS*:

*"Listen, my child, and know my heart. Light draws to light. Dark draws to
dark. Draw in my light. Stand in that light and drink deeply. The light of My
Word overshadows all darkness. Drink deeply and chase away the darkness
with my light, My Word. Strength and boldness come forth from that Word.
Seek my face with greater diligence and be restored to the light, My Word.
Stand in awe at the clarity of My Word in your heart and be at peace as each
piece of the puzzle of your life comes into place. Be at peace and proclaim my
goodness. Now unto him who is able to do above all you ask or think be Glory,
now and forevermore. Amen and Amen!"*

A CHILD OF THE LIGHT

Here is a question that only you can answer: Can God take the darkness out of your life? What we believe is everything, and it determines how we will come out of every trial we face on the earth. How we face our fires makes a difference. If we face them with God's light, we will come through with not even the smell of smoke on our clothing! (Isaiah 43.)

When God created the earth, He started with a ball of emptiness, covered with darkness. The Holy Spirit waited there, knowing that the light was coming, that His Hand of creation would change it soon. Did He not wait for each of us in our own pits of darkness, hovering, waiting for the right time to speak life and light into our hearts?

The born-again conversion experience, the moment that relationship to the Creator is established, is designed to remind us of God's power over anything we face. In that one moment of time, He separated us from darkness, changing our lives forever and literally infusing eternity into our DNA. We are now children of the day (Ephesians 5:8, 1 Thessalonians 5:5) thanks to the love of Christ.

Whatever you are facing today, remember that God separated you from darkness once before. He will do it every time you need Him. In the beginning, He has done it already. You are His beloved, separated from the enemy for all time, called to the light, destined for eternity with Him!

Love, Faye

Day Seventy-seven

"When the master of ceremonies tasted the water that was now wine, not knowing where it had come from (though of course, the servants knew), he called the bridegroom over. 'A host always serves the best wine first, he said, 'Then, when everyone has had a lot to drink, he brings out the less expensive wine. But you have kept the best wine until now!' This miraculous sign at Cana in Galilee was the first time Jesus revealed His glory. And His disciples believed in Him."

JOHN 2:9-11 NLT

EXCERPT FROM ROSALIE'S JOURNAL:

"The best is yet to come. Be lifted up this day, released from bombarding afflicting spirits that harass and rob your peace. Be set free to worship Me in spirit and in truth. The tree of life has become a reality to you and with that reality comes a greater responsibility to truth. Look to Me for that truth and flourish and thrive. Minister that truth to others within the framework of My Word. The heavens await your entering in to proclaim the Glory of God. It's been a rough ride, but you've stayed by my side, my precious Bride. Be not ashamed, for my love and work you have continually proclaimed and applied. It cannot be denied. It is simply that your focus has changed and been rearranged. No longer the people to please and appease, but each moment to seize, for your Lord to please. Go forward this day in this brand new way. Seasons of change have come your way, creating glory in everything you say. For my words of truth you shall continue to speak with beauty and grace, in no way weak. I have said, be strong, be courageous, and you shall prevail as we move together along life's trail."

THE BEST FOR LAST

Are you excited yet about the time in which you live? Are you ready for the things we will face, and the blessings we will see in the midst of it? There are wondrous clues in the Bible, and we are reminded in today's excerpt that the things ahead of us are more awesome than the things behind us.

When Jesus made the wine at Cana, it was the first revelation of His glory—the beginning. He saved the very best for the end of the wedding. They had run out of wine. In the latter days, this reminds us, the really good wine will be lacking. The people of God will be dry and in need of joy. The Bride of Christ will be thirsty for the manifestation of God.

Enter Jesus—within each of us who have the Son of God is the capacity to bring the new wine, the fresh anointing that showers people with joy. They can drink of Him and be refreshed. We get to be the ones who bring the new wine to the party! God doesn't want his wedding celebration to die of thirst or lack in joy—He wants it to be a manifestation of His Glory! And WE get to participate!

The best is yet to come! Get ready!

Love, Faye

Day Seventy-eight

"But the Holy Spirit produces this kind of fruit in our lives:
love, joy, peace, patience, kindness, goodness, faithfulness,
gentleness, and self-control. There is no law against these things!
Those who belong to Christ Jesus have nailed the passions and
desires of their sinful nature to His cross and crucified them there.
Since we are living by the Spirit, let us follow the Spirit's leading
in every part of our lives. Let us not become conceited,
or provoke one another, or be jealous of one another."

GALATIANS 5:22-26 NLT

EXCERPT FROM ROSALIE'S JOURNAL:

*"It is a process, child, to bring you into my will and way by your choice and
love. Continue on with steadfastness, for I have brought you far and will take
you yet farther, to be an expression of my love and way. Be strengthened in
body, mind, and spirit through the laying down of self. Freedom comes forth
from the laying down of self. Trials and tribulations come to cause you to lay
down self. (Self defines who we are as an expression of our will, but we are to
be an expression of God's love and will.) Confidence in Me is the key, not confidence in thee—not self-confidence."*

THE EXPRESSION OF CHRIST

Sometimes people focus on the gifts of the Holy Spirit, but ignore
His fruits. That's right, the Holy Spirit is a person, part of the Triune,
One God. He is not an "it," nor are His gifts or fruits. The fruits are
attributes of God and the gifts are the works of God. They don't belong
to us. They are expressions of God himself to the world!

John 8:4-11 is the story about the woman caught in adultery. Think
about it—the woman stood bare naked in front of a crowd that not only
was ready to stone her to death, but also ready to condemn Jesus. She
was shaking, embarrassed, expecting to die any minute. The Pharisees
knew that Jesus wouldn't condemn her, as His track record to that point

had been about mercy and grace and loving the unlovable. So the crowd hoped to find a reason to accuse Him to the rulers (verse 6).

Instead of commanding demons out of her, or making a huge production of it, Jesus stooped over and scribbled in the dirt, ignoring both the woman and the Pharisees. When confronted, He simply asked them if they were without sin, and they all slinked off in humiliation. Then He gently released the woman with a quiet admonition not to do it again.

The actual expression of Christ is about love, forgiveness, gentleness, kindness that convicts of sin and gives people a new chance at life. The devil didn't make us do it—we chose to do it, and God now has to redeem us. As we move forward into His arms, He releases us from all the holds of the enemy in our lives. The expression of His love is woven throughout the Bible, if we will study His methods.

One of the most powerful people that Rosalie and I have known over the years wasn't a big name in Christianity. Most people have never heard of him. He was a short little man from Nigeria, Archbishop Victor Onuigbo, who had originally been a medical doctor. In his ministry, God had raised over 200 people from the dead. His churches numbered over 500,000 people, yet meeting him was like meeting your new best friend. He was gentle, kind, and treated everyone equally. He walked in such Holy Ghost power that demons would flee at God's Presence in him. The power in his life was God himself, and he simply stayed out of the way. He could be in the background and didn't have to have center stage, yet you could feel the power of God just standing next to him. He knew how to lay down his own flesh to speak an accurate, powerful word from the Lord. He is now home with Jesus, but we will never forget that expression of God in his heart. And from my own heart, his friendship made a lasting impression on my walk with Jesus.

The most effective ministry, the ministry that stands the test of time, is not ministry done behind the microphone or in a big meeting—it is the personal relationship that walks together through the fires of life. Rosalie and I have walked through many fires together. We have shared God's love, His gentleness in the midst of fires that would normally break people from Jesus forever. It is the expression of Christ that we have shared day by day with each other and with the heart friends that has kept us in His heart and in His will. It is the sharing of God's attributes with those around us, and allowing the work of God to move through us unhindered by our own stuff that is at the core of His will for us. It's not about us, it's about God and Who He is.

Love, Faye

Day Seventy-nine

"He heals the brokenhearted and bandages their wounds.
He counts the stars and calls them all by name.
How great is our Lord! His power is absolute!
His understanding is beyond comprehension! The LORD supports
the humble, but He brings the wicked down into the dust."

PSALM 147:3-6 NLT

EXCERPT FROM *WHEN GOD SPEAKS TO MY HEART*:

"My child, I charge you this day to know the hearts of those around you. Be sincere and seek to know and love them for who they are. That expression of love will free their lives from fear and doubt. My love will set them free. Be a messenger of my love, joy, freedom, and truth. Restore confidence through Me. Help them to see the potential of their lives in Me. Be a standard of love, freedom and joy. Every time you hug each one and smile at each one, you impart these precious elements of my heart. It is all part of my plan. Love as I love you!"

HEARTS WITH DESTINY

Have you ever had someone totally miss who you were? Their view of you is based on what they think they see, or their inaccurate "prophesying" so they don't catch your heart. It can be devastating.

The sum total of a person is not about what they look like, or even their background, it's about who they are in their hearts. In the Old Testament, we are reminded that as a man "thinks in his heart, so is he" (Proverbs 23:7 NKJV). Sometimes what they think about themselves can be altered by the love of God. But who will share it?

When I was in college, several of my required courses were in the psychology department. My instructor at first made an instantaneous judgment of me based on what I looked like. Based upon that view of me as unimportant, he ignored me through the entire first part of the semester. Trying to talk to him was very difficult. But when test time came, he was shocked to see me get straight A's in his class. By the time I graduated, he had not only repented in front of the class for his view, he took the time to talk to me on a personal level and get to know my heart on things. Ultimately, it was the time he took to do that which literally saved my life at a critical time in my young career.

Rosalie and I often see people make snap judgments of others based on their station in life, or their appearance. We often see well known people elevated to pedestals of honor when 1 Corinthians 12:22-23 specifically says that the ones who are the least important are the ones who should get the most honor. There are people in the Body of Christ, and even in the world, who have great gifts that need to be shared. But without someone to love them into their place, they just wither and die.

In today's excerpt, God asks us to look past what we see and learn of other's hearts. Hear His Spirit reveal their precious destiny. Hear Him reveal how important their place and purpose might be. You might be standing in front of the next David and miss it, because your background says to "read their mail." But in fact they may just need someone to lift them up and help them find what lies within their hearts. It's not about what we think we know, it's about moving people into God's arms and His destiny. Sometimes it's best not to "know things out loud," but to pray and encourage, building up the person past those things into healing and life!

Love, Faye

Day Eighty

"Enlarge the place of your tent, and let them stretch out
the curtains of your dwellings; do not spare,
lengthen your cords, and strengthen your stakes. For you shall
expand to the right and to the left, and your descendants
will inherit the nations, and make the desolate cities inhabited."

ISAIAH 54:2-3 NKJV

EXCERPT FROM *WALKING ON WITH JESUS*:

"Open wide your tent. It is a place of refreshment and rejuvenation and so shall it ever be. Rejoice and be glad in the task I have given you. Resentment and reluctance cause tiredness. I have given to you that you might give without reservations, freely and with joy. Take your rest when I give it without guilt. Know that when the time comes to give out, that you will have the strength and the means. Release unto Me the reluctance and apprehension. Know that each one has been sent for a reason and I shall bless. Rely on Me to bring it forth. You shall see more fruit of your labors and we shall rejoice together."

STRETCHED TENT PEGS

If you've ever been tent camping, you know that the tent pegs must be placed properly or the tent might collapse in the middle of the night. If they are tight, but not too tight, they should withstand ordinary rain or wind. It's not always easy to pull them tight enough, and sometimes the ground itself is too hard to pound stakes into it.

It's been my experience that when God is about to stretch me in new directions, that He begins to task me more and more. Once when I was attending an Assembly of God church nearby, the choir director asked me to play the piano for choir. I had not played musical scores for many years, and the "reaches" for my hands were extreme. I had to stretch the muscles of my hands in order to play the chords in the music. That, coupled with a lot of computer work, and my wrists and joints became inflamed. It was very painful. A local physical therapist gave me some tips on how to mitigate the pain, and finally my hands became used to it and I could play without pain at all. It was a "stretching"—literally—of my abilities!

We can quit when things get painful, or we can allow the Holy Spirit to stretch us into new abilities and strengths. We can make sure our tent is a place of rejuvenation, a place where we can trust that the Lord has given us the ability to accomplish His purpose. We can stretch those tent pegs as far as we can so that our tent will withstand all that life has to throw at us. We can also allow God to create a tent of meeting with Him that is larger and larger with every trial that we overcome!

Our place in history is a tough one. We can run from it, or we can run into it with the joy of the Lord before us. Every day we read or see something in the news that grieves us or we encounter tribulations in our lives that strike fear in our hearts—many run from those things. Instead, ask the Lord to enlarge the place of your tent—the place where you meet with Him, as well as the place where He grants us greater abilities. You are destined to inherit nations and peoples for the Kingdom. Stretch those tent pegs!

Love, Faye

Day Eighty-one

"Oh God, You are my God; early will I seek you; My soul thirsts
for You; My flesh longs for You in a dry and thirsty land where there
is no water. So I have looked for You in the sanctuary, to see Your
power and Your glory. Because Your lovingkindness is better than life,
my lips shall praise You. Thus I will bless You while I live; I will lift up
my hands in Your name. My soul shall be satisfied as with marrow
and fatness, and my mouth shall praise You with joyful lips."

PSALM 63:1-5 NKJV

EXCERPT FROM *WHEN GOD SPEAKS TO MY HEART*:

*"My child, my heart croons over you like a song of love, the melody sweet, with
the fragrance of Heaven. Can you not hear it within, eliminating all stress and
fear? Listen with your spirit. Open your heart to rejoice in the love I have for
you. My heart yearns after you that you would know Me more intimately. Bask
in the warmth of my love, positioned in the assurance of my promises. My love
is a shield to you. My hand is upon you to bless you. The beauty of my love is
real, and in Me there is a place of quiet, safe rest."*

LOVINGKINDNESS

When the Bible talks about God loving to give us the Kingdom, or
that He loves us abundantly over all that we can ask or think, we usually
have no clue what that means. We get little snatches, but we only know
things in a three dimensional world that we see, touch, and smell. But
our God is multi-dimensional. And He is real. Sometimes we forget!

In the midst of an exceedingly stressful few weeks, God brought the
most wonderful love-touches to my life. My love for Him grew deeper
and He became more real. I knew all that before, but somehow His
manifestation of special love transformed my view to a deeper one. And
He wants you to know that intimacy and transformation is for everyone!

One weekend I saw an oil painting at a local art show of a tugboat
that my father built. It was a huge blessing that touched my heart, but

no way could I afford to purchase it. A couple of weeks later, my next door neighbor, Bev, walked into my home carrying that very painting, and gave it to me as a gift! It hangs in my living room as a reminder that God hears every whisper in our hearts. It is a reminder that no matter what I have been through or what I have lost, God knows everything and will be there for me through it all.

One Saturday, I spent all day trying to catch up on the cleaning in our home. I had run out of ideas for dinner, and had no clue what to fix. So I simply asked the Lord if we could go out to dinner. We didn't really have the money to do so, but I asked Him anyway. Silly little thing, right? God doesn't care about that stuff? Wrong—when my husband came home from his market trip to sell rocks, he walked in the door and said, "We're going out." So we went out to dinner because God had blessed him with just enough extra money for a night out.

There is no substitute for the Living God who loves us so much that even the little things matter to Him. He wants to shower all of us with His love. The world around us is very harsh, but God is all love and peace for His kids. He is as close as a thought, as gentle as a breeze. When He wraps His mighty wings around us, there is nothing that can take us from Him. The world brings tribulation, but it cannot take away our wonderful Savior! So let us praise Him with joyful lips, for His lovingkindness is better than life!

Love, Faye

Day Eighty-two

"But the Lord replied to her, Martha, Martha, you are anxious and troubled about many things; there is need of only one or but a few things. Mary has chosen the good portion [that which is to her advantage], which shall not be taken away from her."

LUKE 10:41-42 AMP

EXCERPT FROM ROSALIE'S JOURNAL:

"Precious and few are those who will sit at My feet and reflect, receive, and release unto Me their time and love. All I require is a willing heart. Let Me fill in the gaps. It is a time of reflection and joy to be established in strength and peace. Continue to be found amongst my treasures, sparkling and radiant with my love."

THE VALUE OF A MOMENT

The word "precious," both in the Bible and in the world, denotes the term "rare." Precious stones such as diamonds and emeralds are not cheap and are difficult to mine from the earth. They are expensive because they are special, and the more pure in quality, the higher the price.

Our relationship to God was purchased by Jesus—and we were very expensive. Martha, in today's Scripture, was not plugged in to how precious, how important were the words of Jesus. She was too busy doing stuff. How often we, too, are simply too busy to listen to Him. We don't understand how rare, how priceless is the gift He has given us!

I have a friend whose son asked her to go get gas with him one day. Seemed like something unimportant, right? She could have told him to buzz off because she was busy, but she went with him. The very next day he died in a tragic car accident. She showed her son that he was valuable to her, and in so doing, it gave her one precious moment that she will never forget. Do we show our God that we value time with Him?

Rosalie is fond of saying that our relationship to God was not "meant to be a monologue." We get to talk to Him, but He loves to talk to us! Being friends of God, as Abraham and Moses were, requires taking the time to sit before Him, placing rare value on what He has to say. It requires keeping our hearts ready so that these reflective times are filled with His joy, strength, and peace.

Valuing God is important in our lives. If we don't value time with Him, then we really don't appreciate Him! He is priceless, rare, above everything of beauty on the earth—the value of one moment with God is worth more than all the other moments of our lives. Let's take every moment we can!

Love, Faye

Day Eighty-three

"The thief does not come except to steal, and to kill,
and to destroy. I have come that they may have life,
and that they may have it more abundantly."

JOHN 10:10 NKJV

EXCERPT FROM *WALKING ON WITH JESUS*:

"The Christian world has feared and rejected. I fear not and reject not. I give, forgive, and restore. Do as I do! Restoration is my gift to you. Would I not do for you what I expect you to minister to others? I give that you might give. Receive and give. Receive and give. It is a never-ending cycle of love."

THE TIME TO RESTORE

Who hasn't lost much in pursuing the Kingdom? Many of us have lost families, homes, friends, finances, you name it. When difficult situations come, we expect more bad things, and especially in dealing with people. Let's just say that fear of being hurt one more time tends to be our prayer foundation, and it nearly always leads to rejection—of us or them. It's time to "change the channel" in our thoughts! It's time to start doing what God does instead of what our minds tell us. It's time to believe in God's restoration for our lives and the lives of those around us!

If you read the Old Testament, specifically the books of Deuteronomy and Leviticus, you will find numerous references in the Law to situations that require restoration of property, of livestock, or of life. Anything taken must be restored. The good news is…drum roll… JESUS is the FULFILLMENT of the Law! (Matthew 5:17.)

The Body of Christ tends to be reactionary, rather than proactive. (Big words, sorry). That simply means that we often encounter situations or people that make us cringe, and rather than releasing God's restoration into the situation, we condemn or try to control the people. Neither of those two things is productive, and both of them have led to a huge disillusionment with the church at large.

Joel 2 tells us that God will restore what has been destroyed. The Lord said that He is the "Repairer of the Breach"—not just between man and God, but in all areas of our lives. The Lord is about fullness. His glass is never half empty, it's always full and running over. (Psalm 23.) He allows us the privilege of being in His stream of restoration. When we pray for others, we shouldn't try to control the situation in fear, but instead should start releasing God's restoration into them!

Let's live there. When trials come, live in His Presence, feel His love, know that He restores. If He can save our souls, He can restore our lives. If He can change our hearts, He can bring refreshing and hope to us. We will have to walk through some valleys, but His restoration, His abundance is a promise we can count on. And when we give that gift to others, their walk in Christ becomes strong and stable. We are building a strong Kingdom of God, one restored heart at a time!

Love, Faye

Day Eighty-four

"And Moses said to the people, 'Do not be afraid.
Stand still, and see the salvation of the LORD, which
He will accomplish for you today. For the Egyptians
whom you see today, you shall see again no more forever.
The LORD will fight for you, and you shall hold your peace.'"

EXODUS 14:13-14 NKJV

EXCERPT FROM ROSALIE'S JOURNAL:

*"Past sorrows are no more—up in a puff of smoke. Before you is the Red Sea
with the sun shimmering upon it at evening. You shall walk straight through it
on dry land, into the land of promise of the new day, resplendent with the blessings of my heart. Repent of the fear of reproach. Fear not, but walk with
strength and faith that you do hear and you do walk in my wisdom and discernment. Go forth in faith. Be strengthened in my love."*

THE RED SEA AND THE PROMISE

Do we have the faith to leave the comfort of our Egypts, and follow
God to the Promised Land? In spite of the obstacles? In actuality, few
of us have that kind of faith. We say to ourselves, "It's comfortable here.
Yeah, the brick-making is hard, and I have splinters from the basket
weaving, but at least I don't have to depend on God for my food."

Seriously, have you ever thought about it?

The Red Sea paints a very spiritual picture: it depicts the Blood of
Jesus that washes away all the old things. Pharaoh depicts the enemy of
our souls. The Promised Land is our destiny, and our ultimate eternal
relationship with God. We must grab the faith that moves forward and
walk through His sacrifice to obtain freedom from all that has kept us in
bondage. That can be anything from obvious things like sins (addictions,
etc.) to attitudes and doctrines of men. Those things bind us and keep us
from moving, either by intimidation or just plain fear.

The Red Sea is a promise of dry land, of freedom, of hope for the future. The Blood of Jesus is the fulfillment of that promise!

The Israelites murmured and complained the entire trip to the Promised Land and when push came to shove, after all of the miracles they saw along the way, they were still scared of the giants. Only two men from the original group entered the Promised Land and won the battles!

Not many will move into all that God has for them, because it's easier to stay put. Moses moved forward in spite of what he saw because he believed God. Do we believe Him? Do we hear the threats of our enemies and stay stuck on the shore, or do we hear the whisper of the Lord of Hosts and step right into the water? For those who will follow, the Red Sea really does have the "sun shimmering on it at evening," the Promises that are "yea" and "amen" from the Son of God!

Love, Faye

Day Eighty-five

"Be strong and of good courage; do not be afraid, nor be dismayed,
for the LORD your God is with you wherever you go."

JOSHUA 1:9 NKJV

EXCERPT FROM *THE SINGING BRIDE*:

"My ways are unperceivable to those floating along the sidelines, but many times I have shown you the beauty of My Kingdom and you have been delighted. Now I shall show you what it means to be my disciple, steadfast, immovable and unafraid. You shall see more than you have seen in a lifetime and shall remain unruffled in the shadow of my wing, for my pinions shall protect you, uphold you and show you the way. Many shall be the upheavals, but nothing shall cause you defeat. Resting in the power of your Maker and Friend shall bring you through and you shall know the sweet savor of victory. Defeat shall be unknown to you, for I have made of you a strong and sturdy warrior in My Kingdom. Your feet are shod with granite and your heart is warmed by my love. Your buckler and your shield have I woven together with your praise and thanksgiving. So stand up and be counted in My Army. Go forth with My Banner waving in the breeze and I shall make of you my servant, in whom I am well pleased. I shall send you forth with pride, and we shall prevail. Together we shall sow seeds of peace where there is only frustration, and seeds of love and concern to the cut off, isolated, and brokenhearted."

THE UNRUFFLED WARRIOR

In the first chapter of Joshua, God tells him THREE times within the first nine verses to be strong and courageous. Our God expects us to be unruffled warriors, refusing to be afraid as we move forward in our lives. Thank the Lord He gave us grace, because we aren't really very good at it!

God wants mature heirs, not people who run away. He wants people who will stand in the strength of His Spirit in our difficulties and not give up. How will we "rule and reign" with Christ if we can't stand up in the things we face now? The gift of faith for overcoming is ours just for the asking!

My husband and I once went to the High Sierras in California to go camping and metal detecting. My husband's friend Jerome took his pickup because we decided we didn't need two vehicles. As we climbed the winding dirt road higher and higher, Jerome noticed that his steering was becoming more difficult. Just as we rounded a very steep portion of the road (at the edge of the mountain, no guard rails, no shoulder, straight down several thousand feet), we felt a jerk and heard a clank. The truck careened out of control toward the edge of the road! We prayed, and the truck came to a stop at the absolute ONLY place on the road that had a small wide spot! Inches from certain death, God saved us. We had broken the driveline. God's Faith caused us to kick into prayer, and peace flooded over us. We coasted down the mountain to Truckee, California, and got a new driveline installed.

The gift of faith is not something we can work up, it is given to those who believe and know that God is their protection and redeemer. We are not ruffled in tribulation when our hearts know the King of kings will never leave us. He can work out anything. Nothing can stand between us and God's love. Joshua was the victor over Jericho because he believed God. If we will but refuse fear, believe our Savior, and move forward, all victory will be ours! I want to be an unruffled warrior, how about you?

Love, Faye

Day Eighty-six

"You shall also be a crown of glory in the hand of the LORD,
and a royal diadem in the hand of your God. You shall no longer be
termed Forsaken, nor shall your land and more be termed Desolate;
but you shall be called Hephzibah, and your land Beulah; for the
LORD delights in you, and your land shall be married."

ISAIAH 62:3-4 NKJV

EXCERPT FROM *WALKING ON WITH JESUS*:

"Many times I have cradled you in my arms and comforted you. Many times have you looked to Me to rescue you and tenderly protect you. Know that I have not wavered from my promises to you. One by one they have found a place in your heart, and you have believed with an unfaltering belief. These are my gifts to you: strength in the midst of the storm, light in the midst of the dark, and hope that transcends all doubt. Surely my lovingkindness has led you and protected you. So now go forth unafraid, rejoicing in my might, for it is yours—perceiving, receiving, and committing all that you have and are into my loving care. I have brought you into the vast and unending knowledge of my love for you. Go forth with joy. Go forth with soundness and wholeness of heart, for I am with you."

GOD, KING, BRIDEGROOM

Today's Scripture is about redemption—of our personal lives, of our personal country (land), of our futures. It also makes a point of talking about marriage. But why? Because there is a marriage between God and His people that takes place at the moment we are born again. It changes everything, or it should.

I had a dream one night that poked my curiosity. In it, there was a huge, unending building that had different floors with a seemingly endless amount of rooms on them. There was one giant sized beautifully decorated auditorium—a place where weddings took place. Every outer room was assigned to the brides, bridesmaids, or the groomsmen. Each person had a specific place to be, with specific garments to wear.

The bridesmaids and groomsmen were hired and paid according to the company policy. If anything changed the plans of the couples getting married, the pay would be adjusted accordingly... downward.

I was assigned a deep fuchsia colored dress, the only one in the entire building (not my favorite color, I might add), but they failed to tell me which room to dress in. So I wandered in and out of several places to find the right room. It struck me that the folks in the rooms I visited were extremely sad because they were not the groom or the bride. They were just the hirelings.

Since the dream was so intense, I asked the Lord what in the world He was trying to say. Here is what He told me:

Much of the Body of Christ operates as hirelings rather than brides. They are so involved in programs and their own kingdom-building, that they don't stop to get truly related to the Bridegroom. It's a job that brings in money and personal success, not a relationship that brings in transformation and joy. The brides exhibit joy, the hirelings will not have it.

I asked about the color of the dress I was given in the dream. Fuchsia is a mix of red for the Blood of Jesus and blue for the heavenly realm—sometimes referred to as the prophetic realm. God gave me that color in the dream so that I could discern the hirelings from the bride as I visited the different rooms. Sometimes it is hard to tell the difference—and it takes the gift of discernment to see!

Why did the pay go down when plans changed? Because the only pay the bride should be concerned with is the marriage. Any other focus makes one a hireling, not a bride. Let's just say that we all should not be "gold-diggers," but pure, loving brides of the King.

We must relate to our God in the most personal way. He doesn't want religion, He wants relationship. He doesn't want followers, He wants friends. He doesn't want sacrifice, He wants compassion and generosity. For all of us, including myself, let's dump anything that might make us hirelings. For you men out there, it simply means that even if it is hard for you to get close to others, get close to the Lord. The marriage of the Lamb is coming!

Love, Faye

Day Eighty-seven

"For behold, the darkness shall cover the earth, and gross darkness the people, but the LORD shall arise upon thee, and his glory shall be seen upon thee."

ISAIAH 60:2 KJV

EXCERPT FROM *A WALK WITH JESUS*:

"Manifest my love in such a way as to overshadow the gathering gloom. Light and bright shall my love emanate from you, as to shine through gathering clouds and make them as if they were not there. Mountains shall become molehills in the light of my love for you. I fashion for you an oasis in the desert, a refreshing from my hand to bring you assurance and tranquility. Rest assured, my child, all shall be well, for all is fashioned by my hand for you and unto you. The shoe shall fit like a glove. The shoe of my making shall fit you with ease. The Master Builder has fashioned for you an oasis in the desert, resplendent and complete. Be refreshed. Be at ease, and be at rest in my love."

TURN THE LIGHT ON!

Several years ago, I remember Rick Joyner telling an International Aglow Conference that "God doesn't give His anointing and power in a vacuum. He gives it when it's needed." When things happen, God is there with His power and anointing in abundance. As the Psalms proclaim, He is a very present help in times of trouble.

God's Love, Light, and Truth are available for the times when we need Him the most—they penetrate darkness and break off evil by the very nature of God himself. WE can't do that, but He does it through us. All we have to do is exercise the authority that Jesus gave us!

Once when I was in a foreign country (it was my first time alone in an unfamiliar nation), I sat in my hotel room in total fear of going outside. People stared at me and followed me around, as my white skin and yellow hair were a novelty there. I almost panicked at the thought of going out, yet I knew that if I didn't I would not accomplish what I was sent there to do. After the first week of fearful worry, I finally got off my couch and headed outside to the real world. The turnaround was amazing! Suddenly people were friendly instead of weird, and I made many friends even on the first day out! The Lord brought me numerous Spirit-filled Christians to pray with, and by the end of my stay I had not only accomplished what I set out to do, but was blessed beyond measure with new friends and wonderful opportunities to spread God's love. But it took confronting my fear to release the Light!

Jesus said that He came to "destroy the works of the devil." He made a public shame of the enemy by paying the price for everything we have ever done. Legally speaking, we are free of any "liens" against us. That freedom brings with it the privilege of confronting the enemy whenever he rears his ugly head. (Luke 10:19.) When you are in a spiritual battle (and you know that by the bad feelings that try to snuff out the love and light inside you), the power of God is at your disposal to put an end to it. Your own victory is like a beacon to others!

As the earth grows more and more full of gross darkness, the more the Holy Spirit will rise up within us. Daniel 11:32 says that those who know their God will do exploits—all we have to do is KNOW Him, and He will take care of the rest. Like it says in today's excerpt, the mountains get smacked down and the clouds are penetrated by the Light of Heaven.

We just have to be willing to allow Him to move through us! Turn that light on!

Love, Faye

Day Eighty-eight

"But Christ, as the Son, is in charge of God's entire house.
And we are God's house, if we keep our courage
and remain confident in our hope in Christ."

HEBREWS 3:6 NLT

EXCERPT FROM *WALKING ON WITH JESUS*:

"Soar forth! Soar forth! Readiness to do my will is the prerequisite for my perfect will to come forth. Be not afraid to step forth with confidence and soundness of step, for I shall guide you and lead you to know how you shall proceed. Gradualness is a virtue and is my leading for you. Preparation is the key to success. Bring forth your storehouse of knowledge as brought forth by Me. Be prepared! Be prepared to know my will at every turn. Confidence! Confidence is my word to you this day. Look up and rejoice at every turn in the road. My way for you is steady plodding, step by step."

MOVING FORWARD

One thing I have noted over my lifetime is that traffic is a perfect picture of the reality of life.

One day I drove to Wal-Mart and was literally cut off numerous times by people who failed to obey the traffic rules. If the arrow pointed one direction, they drove the opposite, nearly smacking into those of us who followed the road properly. Then there were the red light runners, who couldn't have cared less about others. They were in such a hurry, they plowed through the traffic regardless of the law. Then there were the impatient drivers who couldn't seem to sit calmly in the line of traffic if there was an accident or construction blocking the road. They were constantly getting out of the line, trying to go around, or zooming backwards in a vain attempt to go in some other direction. Don't you just want to give them a tongue-lashing? (Oh, that would be me…sorry.)

Today's excerpt speaks of a gradual progression, born of preparedness and having the confidence to move forward. God moves us into our destiny at the exact right time and place—when we are ready. When that time comes, we need confidence in Him and the courage to trust Him. There will ALWAYS be those who fail to follow the rules and try to cut us off, endanger our walk or our positions, and try to take our place in the pathway. No matter how many people get in your way, it is God who has the final say!

Over the years in ministry, people have literally tried to shove me out of different places of service and every time, God was my vindicator and help. But I had to have that CONFIDENCE to know that He would help me! If you give in to the people who are "driving badly," you are not holding fast to God's anointing in your life. You must know when someone is trying to run you off the road, and follow God's directions. Preparedness and confidence will help you make the right choices. Others may be impatient or jealous, but like being stuck in a traffic snarl, you can be at peace knowing the result will all come down to the Living God in your life.

When God has given us a gift, a position, or an anointing, we must hold on to it until God's timing. We must VALUE it! If we are called to be leaders, we must not let go of that place just because there are people who want our calling and try every manner of nastiness to steal it. Remember this: traffic violators will eventually have an accident because they are disregarding the safety of others. People who usurp God's anointed will not prosper and that which they try to steal will fall to the ground. You are God's anointed, called and equipped for the special task He has given to you!

Love, Faye

Day Eighty-nine

"Fear not, for I have redeemed you; I have called you by your name;
you are Mine. When you pass through the waters, I will be with you;
and through the rivers, they shall not overflow you. When you
walk through the fire, you shall not be burned, nor shall the flame
scorch you. For I am the LORD your God, the Holy One of Israel,
your Savior; I gave Egypt for your ransom, Ethiopia and Seba in
your place. Since you were precious in My sight, you have been
honored, and I have loved you. Therefore I will give men
for you, and people for your life. Fear not, for I am with you."

ISAIAH 43:1-5 NKJV

EXCERPT FROM *WALKING ON WITH JESUS*:

> *"Stand firm, my child, in the solid foundation of my love and freedom. You have walked many a weary mile. Now stand firm and rejoice in the sure power of my promises to you. The flood tide of the enemy has ravished, but the flood tide of My Spirit shall restore and make new. Stand, my child! Stand and rejoice in the fulfillment of My Word!"*

STILL STANDING!

The world is a harsh place, and ever-increasingly so. Many of God's precious saints are in the fires of trial and tribulation. Within one hour one day, for example, I had three people say the words "life is really hard right now." This makes it ever more important that we encourage one another and pray.

One of my favorite chapters in Scripture is Isaiah 43. In it, God is very honest. No sugar coating. He tells us there will be things to overcome, but He also reminds us that He is with us through it all. There are a couple of tips to help you remember that He isn't ignoring your struggle:

1) Faith believes that "I can do all things through Christ who strengthens me." (Philippians 4:13.) That means even if we are facing death, God not only dwells in us, but comes alongside us

to grant us strength. We will survive. We will overcome. He is God Almighty, Maker of Heaven and earth. Nothing is too hard for Him.

We are destined to see Him work in ways the people of the Old Testament could only see afar off (Hebrews 11).

2) Look in the mirror. Are we having a pity-party, or walking in faith? Why are we alive now instead of a hundred years ago? Was it an accident? Did God hit the time button while snoozing and *oops*, here we are? NO!!!

We are here on the earth now for such a time as this. We are here to love on Jesus, to encourage and pray for each other, to do the will of God on this earth, and fulfill all that He has for us to do. If we get stuck in the pity-party mode, we will miss His Voice, His Comfort, His Presence, and we will miss one of the most exciting times of history!

God knows what is going to happen, and He is aware of everything we face. We just need to remember that we are not here by accident, but by design! When things seem to be hopeless, stand in front of that mirror and remind yourself: I can do whatever God asks because He is with me; and I am here by design, so everything He promised will come to pass! As today's excerpt reminds us: "The flood tide of My Spirit will restore and make new."

Love, Faye

Day Ninety

"In You, O LORD, I put my trust. Let me never be ashamed; deliver me in Your righteousness. Bow down Your ear to me, deliver me speedily; be my rock of refuge, a fortress of defense to save me. For You are my rock and my fortress; therefore, for Your name's sake, lead me and guide me."

PSALM 31:1-3 NKJV

"And we know that all things work together for good to those who love God, to those who are the called according to His purpose."

ROMANS 8:28 NKJV

EXCERPT FROM *WALKING ON WITH JESUS*:

"When you feel the blow of defeat, I always turn it to victory. Time after time, I have been to you the Rock of Gibraltar, being that strong bulwark of peace and stability. I am your stronghold and I will not forsake you. Take on a new identity in Me, Jehovah-Jireh—Jehovah will provide."

A BRIGHTER FUTURE

Some time ago, I found a very old photograph of my dad and mom when they were first married in the 30's. Both of them were very young, very attractive, and they looked extremely happy. As I thought about a time in their lives that was joyful and brimming with hope for the future, it occurred to me their dreams had struck serious obstacles: World War II, economic recessions, depressions, loss of children, etc. The joy faded, and the struggle began soon after they were married. By the time I came along, they were locked in a struggle for survival. I never saw the lightness and joy present in the photograph.

All of us must face the faded dreams of our hearts. We get married with great hope, or we look forward to our children's success, or our desires for the future reach for the sky. And then life happens. While we are on the earth, both our flesh and our enemy rise up and make obstacles that try to steal our dreams and hopes, leaving behind discouragement or even despair.

As Christians, we have something that the world does not have: personal help from Almighty God. That doesn't mean we can do what we want, but it does mean that no matter what happens to us, God will turn it to something that favors us. Even if we lose everything, God will restore to us. Even if we lose our relationships, God will help us have faithful ones next time. When it looks the darkest, trust the Lord.

Jesus told us that He came to destroy the works of the devil. He came to revamp the devil's plans to steal, kill, and destroy and to bring abundant life instead (John 10:10). It's like a seed planted in the ground—first the seed dies and then a new plant comes. When Jesus died and rose for us, resurrection power was released in our lives. When the old dreams die, resurrection and restoration of something better comes!

Today, let's take on a new identity in God—let's believe in Jehovah-Jireh, the Provider; Jehovah Rapha, the Healer; and Emmanuel, God with us. He really is our rock and fortress! He has a special plan for each of us to redeem, restore, and resurrect that which was lost!

Love, Faye

About the Authors

Rosalie and Faye met each other in 1976 when Rosalie moved to Coeur d'Alene, Idaho. Rosalie's love and belief in her personal relationship to God was the catalyst for Faye to come to Jesus in 1977. They became "heart friends" immediately. When Rosalie started A Company of Women in 1996, she invited a handful of friends to that first meeting around her kitchen table in Post Falls, Idaho. Faye was a part of that meeting. Over the years, through the trials of life, their friendship has grown stronger. In an interesting twist of God's humor, Faye is now Rosalie's pastor as well as her friend and assistant.

Rosalie is the author of several devotional books and is the founder of A Company of Women International. ACW spans many countries from the United States to Australia and Africa. Rosalie is married to a wonderful man of God named Stormy (Robert) Storment. Together, their ministry touches the lives of men and women worldwide through not only Rosalie's books, but also through her international prayer family, PraiseNet. Yearly conferences around the United States have endeared Rosalie and her precious husband to her beloved heart friends.

Rosalie has one lovely biological daughter, Shannette, a son-in-law, Reggie, and four wonderful children that she also shares with her husband, Stormy—Michelle, Bruce and his wife Bernadette, Russell and his wife Stacy, Deborah and her husband David, plus many wonderful grandchildren and many spiritual sons and daughters who adore her.

Faye Higbee is pastor of Raven Ministries in Post Falls, Idaho, as well as an author, worship leader, and editor of PraiseNet. She is married to her beloved Myron, and has two step-children, Dr. Dana Higbee and 1st Lt. Jerry Higbee, daughter-in-law Mindy, and two precious grandchildren, Madeleine and Niesa. Faye serves on the administrative boards of several ministries and as an officer in the local Idaho Writer's League. Her career in law enforcement ended in 2004, and since then she has been full time in ministry and writing books, blogs, and articles, both fiction and nonfiction.

Rosalie Storment may be contacted at rosalieacw@gmail.com. Her websites are: www.rosaliewillis.com and www.acompanyofwomen.org. Rosalie and Faye are also both on Facebook!

The PraiseNet prayer network may be accessed at this address: praisenet@acompanyofwomen.org

Faye Higbee may be contacted at mdnf.higbee@gmail.com as well as at the PraiseNet address.